A
HJ

# Date of Return

# Sounds
# of Railways
## and their recording

Peter Handford

**DAVID & CHARLES**
Newton Abbot   London   North Pomfret (Vt)

British Library Cataloguing in Publication Data

Sounds of railways and their recording.
1. Locomotive sounds – Recording and reproducing
I. Title
621.389'32          TJ608

ISBN 0–7153–7631–4

Photoset by Northern Phototypesetting Co, Bolton
and printed in Great Britain
by Biddles Ltd, Guildford, Surrey
for David & Charles (Publishers) Limited
Brunel House, Newton Abbot, Devon

Published in the United States of America
by David & Charles Inc
North Pomfret, Vermont 05053, USA

# Contents

# Introduction

On a bitterly cold December night the late John Gale, author and *Observer* journalist, stood with me on a hillside above Hawick, listening to a train struggling up the steep gradient from the now abandoned station: 'I never realised before what vivid and varied sounds a train can make,' he said. 'I'll have to write this scene into a book.' Perhaps, had he lived, he might have written this book for me; certainly his enthusiasm for sounds which he had never bothered to listen to before was inspiring, and it is the similar enthusiasm of many other people who, during the past 25 years, have shown an appreciative interest in railway recordings, which has inspired the issue of so many records of the sounds of the steam age and eventually led to the writing of this book.

Some people find it amusingly incomprehensible that anybody would want to listen to records of railway sounds. This book is not for such people; it is for those who find the world of railways, and particularly their sounds which convey so much of the atmosphere, interesting, exciting, or simply nostalgic. Railway sounds have always been all those things to me, since long before it became practical to record them, and it is the sounds of steam age railways during the past 45 years or so, in Britain and abroad, which form the main theme of this book.

The viewpoint of a sound recordist is inevitably different from that of a photographer, as are many of the problems and experiences involved in making recordings; some of the experiences may interest railway enthusiasts and possibly others, and some of the problems may be of interest to those who have listened to records of railway sounds, or have made their own recordings.

The power of sound is consistently overlooked and underrated. It is, for instance, a strange fact that, though blindness is normally a subject for sympathy, deafness is all too often treated with inconsiderate amusement. To be sightless is certainly a tragedy, but to be deaf is surely an even greater deprivation because, whereas a sightless person still has the means to form varied mental images inspired by sounds, anybody deprived of their hearing is denied this, one of the most potent means of stimulating the imagination.

So many people have been of inestimable help in making the railway records and in the writing of this book. Some are directly mentioned in the text; it might be invidious to mention others, but my thanks are due to them all — most of all to the many railwaymen of all grades and nationalities whose work has provided the material for the records and who have so often gone out of their way to be helpful. A great deal has been written and said about the sadness which enthusiasts experienced at the demise of the steam locomotive and the closure of numerous railways; far less has been heard of the reactions of those whose working life was spent on the railways, among steam locomotives, and if they would consider it as a compliment, it is to them and of course to my endlessly patient and long suffering family, that this book is dedicated.

Peter Handford<br>
East Suffolk. Summer 1979

# Chapter 1
# The fascination of sound

The sounds of railway operation, like the sounds of the sea, are so instantly evocative that, for many years, they have been widely used in film and radio productions, to influence the imagination of the audience.

Since the earliest days of film production, directors have made frequent use of the enormous visual potential of railways and particularly the steam locomotive. Originally it was as a simple demonstration of the ability of the film camera to show movement, then to exploit the obvious dramatic potential of, for instance, a heroine tied to the railway lines during the final moments of a serial episode, or the frustration of a villain on horseback, thwarted by the superior speed of a train which, after a thrilling race, beat him to the level crossing. Later, as productions became more sophisticated, images such as thrusting piston rods, whirling wheels, the rise and fall of gleaming connecting rods and clouds of smoke and steam, were more and more widely used, often purely symbolically, to create or enhance a dramatic effect.

The advent of recorded motion picture sound immediately brought a new realism to the visual image and as technique improved, provided a valuable means of enhancing the impact of the image by the imaginative use of sounds which were not necessarily directly connected with that image.

The long, haunting whistles of American locomotives have been heard in countless Hollywood films, in many cases where no train is ever seen on the screen. The sounds of engines, whistles and clanging trucks in a shunting yard; the bustling sounds of a busy station; the shrieking whistle and clattering wheels of a passing express; the slow passage of a distant goods train; all these and many other railway sounds have been used time and

7

again, more frequently than pictures of similar subjects, to set a scene or to create or sustain an atmosphere. Such wide and frequent use of railway sounds is evidence of the influence which they can have on an audience.

The wonderful variety of sounds and rhythms associated with railways have fascinated and inspired many composers. Berlioz, Honneger and Villa Lobos, among others, composed music which had been inspired by railways. Railway rhythms can be found in some of the compositions of Dvořák, who is known to have been a keen railway enthusiast whose students were expected to share his enthusiasm and accompany him to the nearest railway station where, during his visits to America and no doubt in other countries, he spent much of his spare time, between rehearsals and performances, watching and listening to trains.

Johann Strauss junior and Eduard Strauss both composed polkas with railway titles, based on railway rhythms and many years later, in the late 1950s, some very different dance rhythms such as Skiffle were introduced on the BBC Television production *Six Five Special* by a signature tune of the same title, clearly based on railway rhythms and given an added railway emphasis by the accompanying introductory film sequence, which included scenes on the footplate of a steam locomotive.

Duke Ellington frequently worked on his compositions during train journeys, the sounds of which he found inspiring, and more recently such composers as Arthur Butterworth, Ron Grainer and Richard Rodney Bennett have written music which suggests, or is inspired by the sounds of railways. A modern ballet, devised by Jill Gale, was performed in London in 1977 entirely to the rhythmical sounds of various steam locomotives and at a university in Australia, Tristram Cary is working on some compositions in which railway sounds are integrated with more conventional types of music.

This considerable interest of musicians is not in the least surprising, because railway sounds themselves possess many of the attributes of music, the definite rhythms, some simple others more complex; the controlled power and a great range of contrasts in tempo and intensity are all there in railway sounds, just as in music and can be equally worth listening to for their own qualities.

The sounds of a train climbing through the countryside, for instance, can be likened to a symphony in three movements, played without a break: first, pianissimo, the birdsong and a distant whistle emphasise the silence out of which the train is heard approaching, perhaps with a brief and abrupt change of tempo when the wheels slip; the train comes closer at a steady and now slower tempo, reaches a crescendo as it passes by, then climbs away into the distance, now pianissimo again, with maybe a long, lonely whistle as a coda. Sounds such as these are surely as evocative as a musical composition and can be equally emotive; certainly they are a most worthwhile subject for recording and for the production of a series of gramophone records.

Records of railway sounds are sometimes referred to as Train Noises; this can be deliberately derisive but is more often simply thoughtless. No sound recordist will be pleased if his recordings are called noises, unless he is doing some work for the admirable Noise Abatement Society. The distinction between sound and noise is important, though sometimes hard to define; generally a sound which is unpleasant or objectionable to the listener is called a noise, therefore one person's sound can obviously be another person's noise. The merry toots of a car horn in a street, late at night, may be a cheery sound to a motorist leaving a party, but it will be an intensely irritating, unnecessary and illegal noise to all those woken by it; the new motorbike, roaring up and down the road, delights the rider with its powerful sounds while the residents are infuriated by the noise; the extravagant Concorde may sound splendid to a jet set executive cossetted in a soundproofed cabin but it makes a painful and possibly damaging noise for those unfortunate to be anywhere near the flight path.

Certain sound is always described as noise – the penetrating stab of pneumatic drills for instance. The noise of pneumatic drills, at work near Big Ben, was one of the sounds which delighted listeners to an early recording produced to demonstrate the wonders of stereophonic sound! Perhaps the

9

noise of juggernaut lorries, so intensely irritating to unfortunate victims living alongside through roads and motorways, is a delightful sound to road transport interests.

Noise is one of the most evil and intrusive pollutants of modern life and it is sad that it is given so little consideration by politicians and planners. Aircraft and heavy road vehicles are among the worst and most persistent polluters, by comparison with which the noise caused by any railway is insignificant. The publishers of this book occupy offices adjoining Newton Abbot railway station, on the West of England main line; in such a situation it might be thought that the noise of the railway would be most disturbing. However, although there obviously is noise from the railway at times, it is always of short duration and is much less intrusive than the endless and variously irritating noise from the roads.

Even in times when railways carried much more traffic than they do now and steam trains on jointed track were noisier than those with electric or diesel traction on welded rails, the noise from a main line was only intermittent, of short duration and because of its different nature less excrutiating than that of aircraft or road vehicles. The making of recordings for railway records, at such remote locations as Barkston or Shap Wells, which was then far from a motorway, provided opportunities to compare the type and amount of noise created by road and rail traffic. The ceaseless grind of whining lorries on a main road, some miles away, often formed a continuous background to the silence of the lineside at such locations, particularly during the night; the railway, in contrast, was completely silent except during the brief passage of trains carrying many times the load of the intrusive road vehicles.

Sometimes, if the wind blew from the direction of the road, recording at such locations became impossible and at other locations, such as the climb to Beattock summit, it was virtually impossible at any time, because the incessant racket from the road drowned the sounds of the trains, even those with two hard working engines, except during the short time when the train passed by.

The pollution of aircraft noise is even more intrusive than that from roads, spreading over a wider area to the remotest places. Aircraft noise is one of the worst problems which a sound recordist has to face, for it is quite unpredictable and no location can be considered safe from it since, in places over which commercial aircraft seldom fly, the armed forces, immune to most criticism, may ensure that silence is regularly and brutally shattered. Usually they choose the normally most peaceful and naturally most beautiful areas, such as Wales, Yorkshire, the Cotswolds and East Anglia, over which to make the most hideous noises at the lowest possible altitude.

Modern railways are most concerned about noise and its effects on passengers and the environment. ORE, an international test and research organisation of 43 European railways, with headquarters in Utrecht, is at present investigating ways of reducing noise. Unfortunately there is little evidence that any similar concern is shown by road or aircraft operators, unless, as in the case of initial Concorde landings in America, their operations are directly threatened by excessive noise.

It is impossible to think of a sound which will not become an irritating noise to somebody in some circumstances. Railway sound, like certain forms of music, will be merely noise to some people. They will almost certainly be irritating noises to those who have been subjected to a non-stop nightly performance of shunting sounds within a few yards of a bedroom window, but to any railway enthusiast the various sounds of the railways will be an interesting and evocative form of music. People other than railway enthusiasts usually react to records of railway sounds with, at worst, amused tolerance and rarely with hostility or indifference; even the indifferent can sometimes become interested, if they can be persuaded to read the record sleeve notes which set the scene and then listen attentively to a properly presented sequence of railway sounds. Never having paid much attention to such sounds before, they can be surprised at their reactions. They may find the rhythms interesting, even exciting, or possibly the sounds will recall some past experience; there have been cases of complete conversion from indifference to real enthusiasm.

One of the commonest reasons for interest and enjoyment in listening to railway records is that, because so many people have had experiences which are directly or indirectly linked with railways, listening to these sounds recalls nostalgic memories.

Those who grew up between the wars had the advantage of knowing a country not then widely infested with lorries and aircraft; the everyday sounds were then more distinct and less raucous and it was possible to hear them without being deafened.

Railways were then the accepted way to move passengers or freight and railway journeys were often something of an occasion; the holiday train journey, or the day excursion, was a real adventure for children, so much more exciting than piling into the familiar family car and however long or late the train journey, surely less of a strain for parents than an overnight drive, ending in a traffic jam on a bypass or motorway exit.

There were few places not within reach of railways, which had become an accepted, useful and seemingly permanent part of everyday life. Trails of steam across the countryside were a normal and natural part of the landscape and in the same way the sounds of the railways were a normal and accepted part of the pattern of everyday sounds.

It was strangely comforting to hear a distant train while lying in bed on a winter night and many countrymen made use of the sounds of the railway as an aid to local weather forecasting: 'the trains sound that close tonight, there'll surely be rain before morning.'

To people who knew that period the appeal of railway records will be nostalgic, and for those of a later age the recordings have considerable value in their ability to convey, in sound, the nature of life in the railway age.

Unfortunately the comprehensive recording of the sounds of the true railway age, in the same manner as that scene was so well captured by photographers and artists, was not possible; the tape recorder arrived too late and earlier methods of sound recording were delicate, complex, costly and generally too cumbersome to be used on location, other than for expensive specialised purposes, such as film or radio productions. Fortunately, however, the sound scene changed more slowly than the visual; the addition of a British Railways number and emblem made no difference to the sound of a pre-grouping engine and much of the atmosphere of the steam railway age remained in the sounds of railways in Britain in the 1950s and considerably later in some other countries.

The world of railways has always had much to offer to those who work in it and to the interested observer. It is an individualistic world, somewhat detached and in some ways almost secretive, but the secrets are well worth looking for and railwaymen, who have an interest and pride in their work, can usually be persuaded to share at least some of the secrets with an enthusiast.

Innumerable contrasts — drama, humour, peacefulness, excitement and an inexplicable sadness — all exist in the sights and sounds of the railways. There is the sense of occasion and excitement in the departure of a long distance express train; the peacefully unhurried charm of a rural branch line; the lonely life of the signalman; the enormous power under the control of the engine driver and dependent upon the expertise and physical efforts of the fireman; the drama of an engine struggling with a heavy load in adverse conditions; and the sense of humour of railwaymen, often most evident when things are at their worst. Such things are an inseparable part of railway working, a difficult, dedicated, demanding and sometimes dangerous way of life. The difficulties and demands were certainly at their peak during the steam age, but they can still be evident now in some unexpected crisis, such as the 1978 snowfalls.

Sounds have always been important in railway operations. The bell codes in the signal box are an obvious example; engine whistles also use significant codes, to indicate a train destination when approaching a junction, or between one engine and another in the case of a train with banking or pilot engines. Some engines, on the GWR for example, were fitted with two whistles of different notes, one of which was intended for use only in an emergency. Certain drivers and firemen sometimes used the twin whistles for other than emergency purposes and crews at Aylesbury shed devised a signature tune which was played on the twin whistles of ex GWR engines with varying degrees of skill, and more frequently, used the two whistles to produce a creditable imitation of a lusty cuckoo; such cuckoo notes were often answered by a spirited rendering of the opening notes of *On Ilkley Moor baat'at* when diesel multiple-units first appeared on services from Marylebone.

The whistles of engines, guards, platform staff and shunters and the use of detonators as the ultimate warning of danger, all have their places as audible signals, even when nothing can be seen, and the siren and bell signals of the automatic warning system in the engine cab, a useful aid at any time, become invaluable in such conditions as fog or falling snow.

Sounds are of particular importance to engine drivers, especially on steam locomotives; the sounds of a working locomotive give a useful indication of performance and the various sounds heard from the engine, from the track and reflected from the lineside, all provide an experienced driver with an indication of his whereabouts, particularly helpful at night or in bad weather when, even if he leans out from the cab, the driver's view of the line ahead can sometimes vary only from fair to appalling.

Several drivers, including such well known characters of the steam age as Sam Gingell and Bill Hoole, listened to recordings made from, or near the footplate during various journeys; if they were told the starting point and then listened to the recordings their judgement of location, at any time, was practically infallible, even in some cases when the recording had been interrupted for a change of tape reels. This assessment of location by sounds was not confined to British drivers; a French driver and fireman listened to recordings of their streamlined 4-6-4 No 232 S 002 made during a journey between Paris Nord and Aulnoye and their judgement was equally accurate.

The steam engine, said to be one of the very few inventions which have been used solely for the benefit of mankind, is certainly one of the most individual of machines; it possesses many human attributes and despite its size and strength, is internationally considered to be feminine in temperament. The relationship between a steam engine and driver can be very close, similar to that which existed between ploughman and horse.

14

The steam locomotive must be one of the most widely written about, most frequently pictured and probably the best loved machine which has ever been produced and it is inevitable that steam locomotives should be the star artistes of railway records; they are by no means the only performers, however, for the large and varied supporting cast is also important. The rhythms of wheels over rail joints, points and crossings, the clang of buffers and couplings, the voices of railwaymen and station announcers, particularly when detailing services to stations now long since closed, the whistles of guards and shunters, the clatter of signal arms and the sounds of bells and levers in signal boxes; such sounds as these add atmosphere and character to the recordings of locomotives and trains. The sounds of nature set the scene in the countryside where railways, blending naturally with the landscape, have long offered a natural environment for wildlife, infinitely safer and more agreeable than the verges of a main road, with constant heavy traffic and attendant noise, fumes and litter.

Much of the variety has disappeared from railways in recent years, as have most of the steam locomotives and in this country far too many of the lines. Yet there is still much of interest in the sounds of modern railways, particularly in the differences between old and new, as illustrated in such records as *Changing Trains,* which contrasts the sounds of various steam and diesel locomotives during the transition years, and *This is York,* a record which contrasts the sounds of York Station in the steam age, in 1957, with those of the diesel age, in 1977, the centenary year of the present York Station.

During the making of the 1977 recordings at York there were many contrasts; the greatly reduced traffic on the railway was depressingly obvious and the departure of Inter-City 125 No 254 002 on a northbound crew training run, was smoothly impressive and produced some interesting sounds, but did not really create such a powerful impression as the departure of an A3 Pacific, slipping its heart out with a northbound train, on an equally wet day 20 years earlier. The roar of a diesel locomotive heading a southbound train through the station under the great roof was certainly powerful, but a good deal less graceful and

15

rhythmical than an A4 Pacific doing the same thing in 1957.

There were similarities between 1957 and 1977; Mrs Grace Robinson, the station announcer whose voice was frequently heard during the making of the 1957 recordings, was again on duty in 1977, though she no longer greeted arriving trains with the long-famous announcement 'This is York'. The familiar voice from the loudspeakers did something to create an atmosphere of stability and continuity at York Station, as did the friendly interest and helpfulness of the railwaymen, which was just as welcoming and welcome in 1977 as it had been in 1957.

Given the use of imagination by the listener to the same extent as it should be used when listening to a radio drama, there is no doubt that more of the whole atmosphere of railways can be conveyed by sound recordings than by any other medium; even the sound film, its closest rival, is limited to that which can be seen by the camera and by the comparitively short lengths of time for which the camera can see a moving train. It is a common problem, when matching the sound and the picture of a filmed railway sequence, that the useful duration of the picture is invariably far less than that of the equivalent sound track.

A still picture, however excellent, catches only an instant in time within the limited angle and focus of the lens, whereas a recording, made in reasonable conditions, can effectively capture the whole atmosphere of a location for a considerable time, even when the subject is hidden from view. The absolute angle and definitive focus of a lens does, however, give it a great advantage which is not shared to anything like the same degree by microphones, the ability to exclude completely unwanted objects from the picture.

It was always an exciting and moving experience to spend a night by the lineside, near Ribblehead or Shap, for example, or on the Scottish border, beside the now closed and destroyed Waverley route. Such experiences could only be conveyed by words or sounds, or possibly paintings, since photography or filming would have been impossible without the aid of lights which, even if their use had been practical, would have completely ruined the whole atmosphere of the setting.

Far away an approaching train came out of a silence

16

emphasised by the bleat of a restless, unseen sheep, or the hoot of an owl; there was nothing to be seen until the train rounded a curve from behind a shoulder of a hill, then, from the frequently opened firebox door, there was a sudden glare, reflected from the billowing trail of steam and smoke and indicative of the endless physical efforts of an expert fireman, as the engine plodded up the steep, continuous gradient at the head of a heavy train. Minutes later the train came past, briefly outlined against the night sky, making steady progress until the driving wheels suddenly slipped on the dew dampened rails of a curve; the slipping was immediately brought under control by the driver, fully alert in the middle of the night, after some time already spent on a far from comfortable, noisily vibrating footplate. The engine settled down and climbed away into the distance, towards a signal light which, despite a shrilly protesting whistle, remained obstinately yellow, threatening the possibility of having to make a difficult start from the next signal, maybe even of stalling on the slippery rails of the continuing climb.

On the Central Wales line, when freight trains worked through the night, an 8F class 2-8-0 banking engine assisted heavy westbound trains on the long 1 in 60 climb from Knighton, past Knucklas, to Llangunllo. The sounds of the two hard working engines filled the valley for minutes on end as they slogged up the single line towards the long, curving tunnel through which the line runs over the summit, and then down through a cutting to the tiny station and passing loop at Llangunllo, where the oil-lamp lit signal box was manned day and night. Streams of glowing cinders shot high into the air above the valley, and in the glare from the firebox the crew of the banking engine could sometimes be glimpsed, with scarves or handkerchiefs tied across nose and mouth to give some protection from the impossible atmosphere of the tunnel, filled with choking fumes from the leading engine. Some time after the train had disappeared into the tunnel the banking engine would reappear, now running tender first, and away it went, down the gradient towards Knighton, with clanking coupling rods and wheels making a gentler and totally different sound to the barking exhausts of the climb.

The Central Wales line is still open now, but the freight trains have long since vanished; so much of the power and excitement of their working lay in the sounds, and only by recordings can such scenes be brought back to life.

Equally exciting and in complete contrast, whether by day or night, are the sounds of an express passing at speed with a sudden crescendo, emphasised by the rapid tattoo of wheels over rail joints and points and perhaps by a whistle, changing its note as the engine roars past. This and many other things could be heard at a main line station, such as Hitchin, Bletchley, Templecombe, Basingstoke or Grantham, which, particularly between early afternoon and the early hours of the morning, provided an endless variety of sounds and sights.

There were main line expresses, some tearing past, others stopping, perhaps to change engines, then starting out from the station, local trains, making main line connections, and the various freight yards, gradually coming to life during the afternoon and reaching peaks of frenzied activity as freight trains arrived to detach or pick up wagons. A sudden silence then, as everything seemed to finish at once and nothing much happened anywhere. Soon points moved, signals changed to green and the night mail roared past, lights blazing at the side of the mail vans, from which the mail pouch and net were extended for exchange at the nearby lineside post. A newspaper train followed, made a brief call and started vigorously away from the station, heading north as a southbound fitted freight train rattled past. A tank engine moved some vans towards the station, then the first heavy sleeping car expresses rushed by and away into the darkness out of which a loose-coupled freight train appeared, slowly clanking and squealing to a stop in the down yard, which now came back to life with a good deal of backchat between train crew and shunters.

So much of all this drama, humour and excitement, which is inseparable from the day and night world of railways anywhere, can best and sometimes can only be conveyed by sound recordings, listened to with imagination.

# Chapter 2
# Sounds of war

One of the few compensations for going back to school was that the journey was made by train; one of the even fewer compensations for staying there was the busy railway, from Horsham to Littlehampton and Shoreham, which ran through the grounds and was directly responsible for many dropped catches and missed kicks on the adjoining playing fields. The railway was within earshot of dormitories and classrooms, but not within sight, which was just as well for the academic progress of railway enthusiast pupils.

Railways and steam engines fascinated me from the earliest age and their sounds were always a major part of their attraction. This fascination with sounds and a later developing interest in films gave me the, then very bizarre, ambition to become a film sound recordist. Such a strange idea brought an immediate and strong reaction from the school authorities, who well-meaningly considered that they had more than the normal responsibility for my future, because my father, a country parson from whom I inherited enthusiasm for railways, had, after a long illness, died during my first term at school. In any case, sound recording for films was not one of the professions considered to be suitable for ex pupils.

Strenuous efforts were made to dissuade me from such an unsuitable and impractical choice of career, but each such lecture merely increased the determination and eventually led to obstinate and open rebellion; such behaviour could obviously not be tolerated, so it was decided that something drastic must be done and arrangements were made for a course of treatment by a psychiatrist, who was most intrigued by the case of a stubborn boy with eccentric interests and curious ambitions.

The visits to the psychiatrist were by no means a punishment, for his consulting room was in London and that meant extra train journeys, in school time, to the envy of railway enthusiast friends. The psychiatric sessions were totally ineffective and usually quite short, so that there was often time to spare for some illicit visits to one of the London termini, to see and listen to trains, or occasionally and even more illicitly, for a quick visit to a cinema, before train time; on the train to Horsham, usually hauled by one of the former LBSC Marsh Atlantics, there might be the additional luxury of afternoon tea in the third class Pullman car, if there was any pocket money to spare.

Persistent letter writing eventually brought one or two interviews with film companies and finally, by a lucky chance, the offer of a job in the sound recording department of Alexander Korda's London Film Productions. In the spring of 1936 the school finally abandoned its efforts to encourage the choice of a more suitable career and, to the relief of all concerned, allowed me to leave.

The job, at the then newly completed Denham Film Studios, involved making tea, loading and unloading film magazines for the use of the optical sound recording equipment and being generally useful. At the same time, I was trying to learn, in what was then the only possible way, by experience and example, the elements of the complex science and art of sound recording and the intricacies of the equipment and processes involved in recording and in its application to film production.

Denham Studios had some advantages for a railway enthusiast; they were within sight and sound of an interesting and then very busy main line, labelled on all the noticeboards by its full title 'Great Western & Great Central Joint Committee'. Even the studio grounds had something to offer, for a railway, about a $\frac{1}{2}$ mile long, had been built there, complete with a station which was frequently revamped to suit the setting and period of a particular film, be it English, such as *South Riding*, or Russian, such as the Marlene Dietrich, Robert Donat film *Knight Without Armour*. The line was worked by an ex LNER J15 class 0-6-0 which, like the station, was altered in appearance to suit the film; the shedmaster at Kings Lynn, where the engine had last been based, would never have recognised his J15 when it was

20

credibly made up, in all respects except size and a change of gauge, as a Russian locomotive.

I soon found local digs, as close as possible to the railway near Denham Golf Club Platform. During the $3\frac{1}{2}$ years I spent at Denham the GW&GC line was a constant source of interest, used by a variety of engines hauling heavy traffic by day and night. The erratic hours of work involved in film production gave me opportunities to see and hear the passing trains, even if only from a distance or during cycle rides to and from the studios.

Early one morning the inhabitants of Higher Denham were woken by a tremendous noise from the railway. Naturally this got me out of bed and I hurriedly dressed. In a field of cabbages, not far from Denham Golf Club Platform, a cloud of steam was rising above a GWR 2-8-0 which, while heading an up goods train on the down line during a period of single line working, had left the track at some crossover points; the driver and fireman had jumped clear while the engine pulled most of the train into the field and rolled over onto its side, where it now lay. Unfortunately it was time to go to work at the studios before all the interesting clearing up operations began and by the late evening everything, apart from a number of wagons, had been cleared away.

The hours of work at Denham were long, often excessive, and there were few days off, apart from most Sundays. On Sundays there were many remarkably cheap excursion trains, from London to any number of destinations, even as far as Newcastle-upon-Tyne, with an overnight return, and I spent many free Sundays travelling by train, preferably over a previously untravelled route to the furthest destination that could be reached in a day; the destinations were not always particularly attractive, for there was not a great deal to do on a winter Sunday afternoon in Mansfield, Grimsby, Derby or Kings Lynn. It was often a relief to rejoin the train, but the journey was the main attraction and there was always the interesting variety of engines which hauled the trains or could be seen from them. The loads of these excursion trains were frequently heavy and delays from Sunday track work often added to the hard work and long hours of the engines and crews.

Army call up papers arrived in the autumn of 1939 and soon after Christmas in that bitterly cold winter, the ill-equipped Royal Artillery battery to which I had been posted, sailed from Southampton on the LNER ship *Amsterdam* to join the British Expeditionary Force in France. After some months of inactivity based at a village near Rheims, where we had been taken in a train including some of those '40 men or 8 horses' wagons, German attacks began. After numerous moves around North West France eventually we were ordered on to a coal boat and found ourselves at Southampton to learn for the first time of the evacuation from Dunkerque and of the armistice between France and Germany.

In 1941 the powers that be decided that a film unit should be formed in the army and other services, with the object of making documentary films and photographic records of any future campaigns in any theatre of the war, for immediate propaganda use and future historical records. No doubt the decision was prompted by the fact that the German forces had such units from the very beginning of the war and from material which they supplied a large number of extremely effective propaganda films had been produced and were widely distributed in neutral countries, which were also well supplied with still photographs of German forces in victorious action. As soon as a decision was announced to form a film unit in the British Army, any and all personnel with professional experience in film production, or as photographers, were ordered to report immediately to their commanding officers; I need hardly add that I duly reported! Interviews followed at the War Office and all those selected were then transferred to AFPU, the Army Film & Photographic Unit, which had established its headquarters at Pinewood Studios, which had been requisitioned earlier in the war and were now shared with the Crown Film Unit and the newly formed RAF Film Unit.

After a year or so based at Pinewood, spent mainly in recording sound tracks for various films made up from material sent back by AFPU cameramen, many of whom were already actively engaged in the Western Desert and elsewhere, there came a demand for the training of additional cameramen, who would be required for future offensives, such as the much discussed Second Front. There followed, for all of us who volunteered, a period of training in the use of still and 35mm cine cameras. Those who passed the preliminary tests were then put through various infantry training courses, battle schools and invasion exercises, armed with a revolver, a still camera (made in Germany and captured from intercepted cargo ships) and an American-made cine camera, with the object of learning how to make effective use of the cameras in battle conditions and to produce useful film footage and still photographs, without being a hindrance or becoming a liability to others involved in the operation. The setting up of specially posed or staged incidents, away from the battle area was, at all times, a severely punishable offence.

During the long period of preparation which led up to D-Day there were endless assignments to film invasion exercises and airborne landings, but then came an unexpectedly pleasant assignment to film the movement of equipment and supplies on the railways. This was a wonderful experience and making full use of such a heaven-sent official opportunity, I lost no time in making arrangements for my first properly authorised footplate trips. Footplate passes had to be obtained in the usual way, from the individual railway companies. There was, though, one occasional advantage over the issue of footplate passes in more normal times for it was not always possible to spare from more important duties a locomotive inspector to accompany me on the footplate.

One memorable trip I had was on the footplate of LNER No 8876, a Claud Hamilton 4-4-0, with a trainload of Sherman tanks from Newmarket. The train was so heavy that even after backing up to compress the buffers, the opening of the regulator produced hardly the slightest forward movement; assistance had to be called for and was provided by another Claud, hardly the most suitable engines for such a job, but together they managed it well. The pilot Claud had to be detached at Cambridge, leaving No 8876 to carry on alone. During the subsequent journey south the train had to be divided after a signal check, drawn forward in two separate sections to the next station, reassembled there, and not without effort started on a more favourable gradient; small wonder that wartime trains were subject to unforseen delays!

Another interesting journey in East Anglia was on General Eisenhower's special train, made up entirely of impeccably varnished LNER Gresley stock; a footplate journey was also made on B12 4-6-0 No 2819, which hauled the train once.

On the LMS main line there was a journey on the footplate of a Stanier Black Five 4-6-0 at the head of an army supply train from Willesden to Northampton. This trip produced a great deal of interesting film footage and many photographs of the engine and train and the scenes from it. Because of the incredible density of traffic, in both directions, this train, like others on the freight lines, worked block to block for much of the time and the journey of 60 miles from Willesden to Northampton Castle took no less than *seven* hours.

Even the Shropshire & Montgomeryshire Railway, one of the Colonel Stephens lines was busy with ammunition trains operated by the Royal Engineers, based at Kinnerley where the strange little locomotive *Gazelle*, still carrying S&M lettering, stood on a short siding near the Royal Engineers' headquarters.

This fascinating railway interlude came to an abrupt end on 21 May 1944, when the AFPU detachment moved to Wentworth and from there to a pre D-Day concentration area near Southampton, for attachment to the 4th Royal Marine Commando, with whom we were to make the D-Day landings.

This time there was no train journey after landing in France and apart from the rusty rails of a local line which ran parallel to the beach, it was not until more than a month later, in Caen on 17 July, that I saw French Railways once again.

The destruction in Caen was appalling; the railway station, yards and locomotive sheds were a total shambles of twisted rails which spiked into the air, wrecked coaches, wagons and engines were up-ended, flung onto their sides, or precariously balanced on the edge of bomb and shell craters, filled with water after days of torrential rain.

Eventually the weather improved, as did the military situation when a pincer movement closed the Falaise gap. On 14 August I was in a detachment of four AFPU cameramen ordered to move south through Vire, Fougères, Laval and Le Mans to link up with American army units and then go on to Rambouillet, to join General Le Clerc's Free French Division and move forward with them to Paris, which we entered on Friday 25 August.

The Parisian welcome was ecstatic and unforgettable, but some street fighting and sniping continued sporadically, culminating in an attack on the quite unshakeable General de Gaulle, from snipers high above the square outside Notre Dame, during a triumphal parade on 26 August. Below ground the Metro was running a service and with tickets freely given, like so much else in liberated Paris, it was on the Metro that we had our first train ride since leaving England.

On 28 August we rejoined the British XXX Corps at Vernon and with them pushed on into Belgium, where we were met with another rapturous welcome in liberated Brussels, which we entered on Sunday 3 September.

Trams ran everywhere in Brussels, and in other parts of Belgium there were some much more individualistic and interesting steam trams which hauled trains of four-wheeled coaches and a brake van, along the roadside tracks and along paved streets through towns and villages. There never was time or opportunity to ride on one of those trams which, though their sounds were not particularly interesting, were always a welcome sight.

Back in England it had been decided that sound recordings made on artillery ranges and during battle exercises were not adequate or authentic accompaniment for the sometimes all too realistic film which was being sent back from various fronts by AFPU cameramen. Many war actuality and commentary recordings had been and were being made by the BBC, using portable disc recorders developed by the MSS Company. The BBC engineers contrived to make many remarkably fine recordings on this equipment, but it could be temperamental in such rugged operating conditions, had certain limitations as to sound quality and most restricting drawback of all, the maximum recording time available was extremely limited. The

German combat film units were believed to be recording on film, which gave superior sound quality with a continuous recording time of up to ten minutes, as against three or four on disc.

The Western Electric Company in England offered AFPU the use of a complete set of optical sound film recording equipment which, by the standards of that time, was as transportable as it could be, consistent with good recording quality, and was driven by the minimum possible number of lead-acid batteries in transportable metal cases. All this equipment was despatched to Brussels in the charge of John Aldred, then an AFPU sergeant and subsequently responsible for the recording of many important British films. He was also the author of *Manual of Sound Recording* first published by Fountain Press in 1963. Together we installed the equipment in a suitable army utility vehicle and prepared to record the sounds of battle on 35mm optical film. The first recordings were made at night, with the 53rd Division, during an attack across the Escaut Canal at Lommel, on the Dutch border.

We later saw and recorded the Airborne troops passing overhead on their way to Nijmegen and Arnhem and made many other recordings during the strongly opposed advance along the narrow corridor to Nijmegen. The link up with the Airborne troops at Arnhem was never made; mist settled over the desolate, flat countryside, then came the rains and later snow and ice.

Back at Eindhoven, where unit HQ had been established, a diminutive 0-6-0 tank engine, NS No 7743, shunted busily around the station yards, where it was later joined by two WD 2-8-0s fitted with air-brake pumps. Nobody saw any trains actually leave the yard to go anywhere, but the sights and sounds of shunting were a welcome change from those of battle.

There were all too few opportunities to watch the shunting at Eindhoven during those winter months, in which we recorded the bitterly opposed advance to Venraij by the 3rd Division and the attack on S'Hertogenbosch by the 53rd Welsh Division. Artillery barrages from both directions, flame throwers, tank guns, street fighting and the petrifying sound of 'Moaning Minnies', the German multi-barrelled mortars, all combined to produce a fantastic pattern of sound which often continued for hours on end, day and night. It might then be followed by sudden silence, which was almost more unnerving; sometimes those silences were broken by the howl of a demented dog, or by cries and shouts.

At times the equipment was set up in the basements of ruined buildings, or in dugouts, but this was done only if there was no sensible alternative, because of the obvious possibility of being overrun in such an immobile situation. On another occasion, at the suggestion of and accompanied by the superbly intrepid BBC war correspondent Chester Wilmot, the equipment was set up in a Sherman tank of the 8th Armoured Division in order to make recordings during a tank battle. A locomotive footplate seemed quiet by comparison with that tank; unfortunately all the recordings were useless because there was considerable electrical interference, and little else could be heard but the tank.

A week before Christmas 1944 German forces led by Field Marshall Von Rundstedt launched a surprise offensive against the American forces in the Ardennes. The British 53rd Division was moved south to support the Americans and we moved with it, to make recordings of the sounds of fierce fighting in the deeply snow covered and frozen country around Marche. As the infantry, perfectly camouflaged in hooded white suits, crawled and plodded through the snow, the sounds of shells and mortar bombs which burst among them, and of machine gun and rifle fire from all directions, echoed from the pine-covered hills. In such surroundings and weather conditions the recordings were totally different in character from those made earlier in the flat lands, towns and villages of Holland.

The German offensive in the Ardennes was smashed and in the middle of January 1945 the British XXX Corps started an attack across the Roer in appalling weather conditions; then, when the 52nd Division, supported by the 8th Armoured Division, made a slow and difficult advance towards Heinsberg, we made the first recordings in Germany.

Those recordings in Germany also turned out to be among the last, for it had been decided that the recording equipment had served its purpose in building up a reasonably comprehensive library of battle sound recordings. In February John Aldred returned to England with the equipment, somewhat scarred but more or less intact and I became a full-time cameraman again.

Moving up through Xanten, we sat down and waited to cross the Rhine; the artillery came up behind us, the barrage began and the RAF came over to bomb Wesel out of existence. It was frustrating to be in the middle of this incredible barrage of sound without the means to record it; filming and photography were, though, possible by the practically continuous light from gun flashes, bursting shells and bombs, rockets and tracer bullets. On 23 March, 161 days after D-Day, we crossed the Rhine near Wesel, with the 15th Scottish Division.

Once across the Rhine, although there was occasional fierce opposition, as at Bocholt, the German retreat became at times something of a rout and often we drove unopposed along roads down which straggling groups of German uniformed soldiers hopelessly wandered, waving improvised white flags and helplessly trying to give themselves up to the passing enemy.

At Celle railway station the platforms and yard were littered with the contents of goods trains, which were being eagerly looted by civilians and slave workers, the displaced persons who came from all over Europe; many from Russia were labelled with the word 'Ost'. These bewildered people seldom had any clear idea where they were, or what was happening and when their masters had fled, they had simply picked up their few pitiful things and started walking, anywhere and everywhere.

Near Celle there was Belsen concentration camp, to which all available AFPU cameramen were sent as soon as its existence was discovered. There is nothing that has not already been said about such places as Belsen and in any case, no words can adequately describe it; even films and photographs appeared to be so unbelievably unreal that they failed to capture the full horror and evil of the place and the people who had charge of it. Sound recordings, for once, would have contributed nothing to any attempts to convey the impressions that Belsen made on those who went there, for there was little to be heard. Few of those who were still alive, physically at least, spoke or made any sound; there was no point.

Pushing on to Luneburg we passed shattered goods trains,

some of which carried V2 rockets the length of a large truck. Just beyond Luneburg was the last major river barrier, the Elbe, but we did not cross that until later, by a bitterly contested bridgehead at Lauenburg south-east of Hamburg in the VIII Corps sector, today on the border between West and East Germany.

After a brief dash back to Holland, to cover the final attack on Arnhem by the 49th Division, we returned to Germany in late April, to join the XXX Corps attack on Bremen. The German troops had a disconcerting habit of infiltrating back behind the British advance, but by the third day we had reached the outskirts of the city and cautiously occupied Bremen Neustadt railway station. The station was deserted though, strangely, not too heavily damaged. In the stationmaster's office was a list of railway dialling codes by the side of a telephone; I dialled the code for Bremen Hauptbahnhof, got an almost immediate reply, asked in English what time the next train left for Basingstoke and hung up!

The way in which the German railways had managed to keep going in one way or another was, as we saw later on, quite extraordinary; maybe they were inspired by the exhortation that 'Wheels must roll for the victory', which was so liberally stencilled on railway buildings and rolling stock.

During the final days of the advance through North Germany, towards Kiel, we passed trains of all descriptions – troop trains, hospital trains, passenger trains and freight trains, some of which were protected by light anti-aircraft guns mounted on open trucks. Some of these trains were headed by still simmering engines, usually 2-10-0s, often in surprisingly good condition; in several cases the drivers and firemen were still on, or near their engines.

On 5 May at Kiel, several trains, which included coaches in which some of the windows were understandably devoid of glass, stood under the equally glassless roof of the badly-damaged main railway station, then made cautious exits over the frequently repaired and somewhat uneven track, hauled by such 4-6-0s as 38-1765, or by one of the ubiquitous 2-10-0 *Kriegsloks*.

The whole situation was extraordinarily confused during the

closing days of the war in Germany; there were pockets of unexpectedly strong resistance, usually from isolated SS units, but in contrast there were incidents such as that at Ratzenburg, where five British soldiers in search of billets walked into a large building, which turned out to be full of armed German troops in hiding. The Germans meekly lined up outside, their weapons were collected and locked up and they remained, quite docile, under guard by two men until arrangements could be made to deal with them.

On 3 May there were reports of much coming and going by German officers, seeking an armistice. Emboldened by these reports and by the general confusion, six of us in two jeeps made, on 4 May, what seems in retrospect an incredibly foolhardy and stupid expedition, to Eutin and Plön, twelve miles behind the German lines, where we magnanimously accepted, filmed and photographed the surrender of the towns by the respective mayors, who were extremely relieved that we were, after all, British and not Russian. With the arrival of a German Panzer colonel and his impeccably uniformed attendant officers, all of whom also seemed anxious to surrender, it seemed wisest to retreat before they realised we were on our own and changed their minds. Back at HQ we learned that German radio had reported Eutin and Plön as captured by strong enemy forces, believed to be heading for Kiel! Such is propaganda; it seemed unnecessary and unwise to answer HQ's enquiries as to what possible grounds there could be for the German radio report and by the time the films and photographs told the true story, it was too late for any, fully justified, reprimands.

At 08.00 hours on 5 May 1945 the 21st Army Group was ordered to cease fire; the subsequent silence was impressive, almost eerie. The relief of the cease fire for those who endured the infinitely more appalling ordeal of the first world war must have been far greater and one wondered how they had retained their sanity, while immovably incarcerated in muddy dug outs and water filled trenches, and bludgeoned by an endless barrage of lethal noise.

On 7 May six of us were ordered to leave Kiel in two jeeps and drive north, through Schleswig and Flensburg, accompanied by a German liason officer as far as the Danish border. Having crossed into Denmark we drove on through Odense to Nyborg, from where the $1\frac{1}{2}$ hour crossing to Korsor was made on board a DBS train ferry, accompanied by some rail wagons which had been shunted on board by a smart little 0-6-0 tank engine with an unusually large dome and tall chimney. On 8 May, the day of the armistice which ended the war with Germany, we entered Copenhagen and were given a tumultuous and prolonged welcome.

During a stay of nearly three weeks in Copenhagen we filmed the arrival of General Montgomery for a parade on 12 May and the ceremonial handing over of German naval vessels, which included the pocket battleships *Prinz Eugen* and *Nurnberg*; there was also time to see something of the neatly clean Danish railways and to enjoy a short ride on a train to Helsingor, from where a train ferry crossed to Helsingborg, clearly visible on the shore of neutral Sweden. That crossing was forbidden in 1945, but I made it many years later, during a train journey from Hook of Holland to Roros, in Norway.

After returning to Germany, I spent some time in various parts of the country, photographing and filming such things as the repatriation of vast numbers of displaced persons of all nationalities.

Back in England, in the spring of 1946, the time for demobilisation came eventually after $6\frac{1}{2}$ years in the army and, having gone through the last rites at a discharge centre in Lancashire, I caught a train from Oldham, Clegg Street, to Manchester, London Road, carrying a demob suit and overcoat and armed with a free rail travel warrant.

31

# Chapter 3
# Transacord is born

The final destination for the travel warrant, issued on discharge from the army, was left to the choice of the individual, and during those last free journeys friendly officials usually overlooked all but the most outrageous deviations from authorised routes or accepted pleas of innocent ignorance. Railway enthusiasts had a splendid opportunity to celebrate their freedom by choosing some unlikely destination, which involved the longest possible trip or offered the chance for a leisurely, but complicated exploration of some hitherto untravelled lines. An enthusiast friend, who lived at Twickenham, was not alone in selecting Wick as his destination, but having reached there, after several days and various diversions, he had to use part of his gratuity to get home.

My own rather more conservative choice, which would allow an exploration of some previously unknown lines, was Carmarthen, reached after $2\frac{1}{2}$ days of intermittent travelling from the demobilisation centre at Oldham, via Manchester, Chester, Oswestry, Moat Lane Junction and Builth Road Low Level; at that point there was time to spare to stay on the train to Three Cocks Junction and then return to Builth Road High Level, before continuing the journey over the Central Wales line to Llandilo, changing there for the final 40 minute, $14\frac{1}{2}$ mile journey on the LNW line to Carmarthen.

During that first journey on the Central Wales line, looking at the superb scenery and listening to the Fowler 2-6-4 tank engine, bravely slogging up the gradients from Llanwrtyd Wells to Sugar Loaf tunnel, I wished, not for the first time, that it was possible to make recordings as easily as one could take photographs, and for the same reasons, to prompt memories of such experiences which should never be forgotten.

It would then have seemed a ridiculous dream to imagine that years later I would make recordings on the footplates of 5MT and 8F locomotives making that climb to Sugar Loaf tunnel with passenger and freight trains. Moreover it would have seemed incredibly unlikely that in May 1964 I would be making lineside recordings of some of the last workings of steam locomotives on the Central Wales line. All of those recordings can now bring the long vanished steam locomotives vividly back to life on that line.

Army pay, such as it was, having ceased abruptly, the less ordered realities of civilian life now had to be faced and employment found. Not unusually the British film industry was in an uncertain state; Denham Studios had been taken over by Rank, and London Film Productions had decided to link up with MGM at Borehamwood, but soon changed that plan. However, the much respected Crown Film Unit was still, somewhat uneasily, at Pinewood and offered a job as sound recordist for documentary films, which I gladly took.

Work for the Crown Film Unit provided much valuable experience, on many different locations in widely varying conditions. The range of subjects was equally varied and included an interview with Winston Churchill, testily impatient, and another with George Bernard Shaw, who chose to be filmed in the garden of his house at Ayot St Lawrence; once he had started talking he would not stop, even to allow film magazines to be changed every ten minutes, until a violent thunderstorm finally drowned the endless flow of words and the film unit. Other assignments varied from the recording of music composed and conducted by Benjamin Britten, to location filming at such diverse places as a science laboratory in Bristol, the Lord Mayor's show in London, a village school in Derbyshire, and the interior of a submarine, submerged off the Scottish coast. Sadly, none of the subjects was directly concerned with railways, though I recorded steam locomotives and pithead winding gear when filming at a Nottinghamshire colliery.

Later in 1946 the future of the Crown Film Unit suddenly seemed most uncertain. Fortunately MGM had offered to me what then seemed a wonderful opportunity to be one of its sound recordists and I signed a contract to work at the almost completed MGM studios in Borehamwood, even though it would entail a long and, with petrol rationing, difficult daily journey from and to Princes Risborough where, as far as practicable from London, I had recently managed to buy a house within sight and sound of the soon to be nationalised Great Western & Great Central Joint line.

Listening to the engines, starting away from Risborough – some working up the steep down line because of a landslip – brought more frustration at the lack of any means to make recordings of such dramatic sounds. This frustration was increased by the fact that I spent every day at Borehamwood studios, surrounded by new recording equipment which, because of the vacillations of MGM policy, was completely idle for months on end.

Sometimes it was possible to escape from the strongly security guarded studio around lunchtime and spend an hour or so beside the LMS Midland main line near Elstree station, watching, listening to and sometimes photographing passing trains. The main event for a time was the appearance of the new LMS diesel locomotive No 10000 which, for a while, hauled an express from St Pancras which passed Elstree in the early afternoon. At that time it was a great novelty to see No 10000 hurrying past with seemingly little effort, making an unfamiliar sound. The sight and sound of the diesel was little more than a novelty, which did not compare with the excitement of a Jubilee or a Compound bursting out from Elstree tunnel; certainly none of us watching the new diesel thought of it as a threat to the supremacy of the familiar steam locomotive.

The sterile and demoralising situation at Borehamwood suddenly and unexpectedly changed. One of the first of what was later to become a flood of American films made in Europe was being produced in Rome, where the unit was having serious problems with sound recording. To avoid the expense of sending in American technicians, MGM at Borehamwood was told to send two technicians to Rome to sort out the difficulties, in whatever combination of languages that might be appropriate and available. Naturally I asked if it would be possible to go by train as flying is bad for the ears – mine anyway, but as usual we should have been there yesterday and had to fly. The flight, from Northolt to Rome, Ciampino, with a stop at Nice, took over eight hours.

In Rome the situation was anything but boring, indeed it was totally chaotic, especially so far as sound recording was concerned. The Western Electric equipment had been seriously mishandled by sundry people, who tried to communicate in various languages, and we had to send for new equipment from the nearest source of supply, Switzerland. The film concerned alleged events in the lives of Cagliostro, Mesmer and assorted European royalty, most of whom spoke with strong American accents. The director was nominally Gregory Ratoff, a most likeable but totally unpredictable Russian, much given to shedding tears of alternate joy and rage. The part of Cagliostro was played by Orson Welles, who had his own individual and unusual ideas about the way in which the film should be made.

The originally intended short visit to Rome became a stay of many months, because we were asked to take over the recording until the completion of the film. There was little time to spare from work, not even for proper sleep at times, but Sundays were always free which I usually spent in making a journey on one of the railways out of Rome. Nearly all these lines were still suffering the aftermath of war, as indeed did life in the city. It was not possible to go far in one day, timekeeping was uncertain, and progress over sometimes dubious track was slow, in trains hauled either by UNRRA locomotives, or by one of an assortment of Italian engines, mostly in various states of disrepair.

By 1952 we had moved house to another in Princes Risborough, this time, though, backing on to the GW&GC main line near the London end of the station. It was beside the down line at the foot of the steep gradient from Saunderton, where the up line separates to run on easier grades on the climb into the Chilterns. At that time Princes Risborough was an excellent rural Buckinghamshire railway centre of great interest to any enthusiast. Apart from the Joint line itself, carrying a variety of through trains of both GW and GC origins between Paddington and Birmingham, and Marylebone, Sheffield and Manchester, there were the branches to Watlington, Oxford and Aylesbury. Highlight of the day was the passing of two down expresses within a few minutes in the early evening, the first being the 6.10pm from Paddington and the second the 6.15pm from Marylebone. GC line drivers nearly always ran hard and occasionally the 6.15pm would get to the convergence at Northolt Junction first, where at least one of the signalmen, whose loyalties I fancy sometimes lay more towards his GC origins than his new Paddington Western Region masters, sometimes slipped the 6.15 down in front of the 6.10 from Paddington, against all the standing instructions. One night the pair of trains made national headlines next day when the Ashendon Junction signalman, where the GC line train turned off the Birmingham main line, misunderstood a message as to which one was first and promptly sent the Western's crack evening express for Birmingham towards Sheffield, which then stopped a mile or so beyond the junction and halted the entire service until it could all be sorted out. Then we had a slip coach off the 7.10pm from Paddington, all adding to the distinctive railway sounds which I managed to record in years to come.

Soon after moving house we built a small wooden signalbox beside the line at the bottom of the garden, ostensibly for the amusement of my two daughters. The *I Spy Signalbox*, equipped with one small signal, was often manned to over capacity during school holidays and became well known to passing engine crews who often saluted any occupants with a superb variety of whistles. Those whistles were just some of the many railway sounds we could hear from that house and garden. There were opportunities for photography but, regrettably in retrospect, I seldom made use of them because there was little hope of approaching the superb results achieved by other, more expert photographers of the railway scene. In any case, even the most evocative photograph could not capture the sounds which, to me, convey so much of the atmosphere of the railway. When it eventually became possible not only to make railway recordings but also to issue them on records, Western Region Driver Stone bought one of the records, noted the address on the label and wrote: ' . . . . . there is a small wooden signalbox at the bottom of a garden near Princes Risborough Station. It has a little distant signal which is nearly always off and I wonder if it has anything to do with Transacord. There can hardly be any drivers and firemen on that line who don't know of the I Spy Signalbox – in fact some firemen will call out to the driver "OK, the distant's off" as they approach the little box.' We had been noticed!

During film work on locations in Britain and abroad there were occasional opportunities for recording railway sounds, directly or indirectly linked with the production. The journeys to film locations were still usually by train and the excitingly different sounds heard during trips abroad increased my frustration, because of the impossibility of making personal recordings. I resolved to make such recordings if ever it became possible, but unfortunately by the time I was able to return with practical recording equipment, such things as the steam-hauled Mistral and Blue Train and the double-headed climb to Annecy, had all disappeared with electrification.

On location in France, for the Herbert Wilcox film *Odette*, I made many interesting recordings of steam-hauled trains on the SNCF at Annecy, Cannes, Cassis and Marseilles, though not all were strictly necessary for the film. In England, for another Herbert Wilcox film, *The Lady With the Lamp*, the replica train of Liverpool & Manchester Railway coaches and 0-4-2 *Lion* were brought to Cole Green station, near Hertford, where various scenes involving the locomotive and train were filmed. It is sad that film recordings, unlike those made for the BBC, were seldom catalogued, much less preserved and many interesting recordings, such as those of *Lion,* have disappeared completely.

Other opportunities for recording railway sounds could sometimes be contrived on location, or during the few days at the end of production when recordings were made of any sound effects which might usefully be incorporated in the final sound track. It became something of a joke that the sound effects for films on which I worked usually included a liberal number of railway recordings, not all of which were entirely relevant. It was less amusing when the producers of a film, set in a period well in advance of the invention of railways, demanded an explanation for the prolonged parking of the 5 ton sound truck beside the

East Coast main line near Hadley Wood! The obvious answer that the A4s, A3s and V2s made a magnificent sound as they roared past and whistled into Hadley Wood South tunnel, would have been unwise, but the dubious excuse of recording birdsong among the trees I don't think was really believed. Returning to that remembered location some years later, specifically to record trains, was a disappointment; most of the Pacifics had been fitted with double chimneys, the trains were lighter and less frequent and there was an endless background of irritating noise from increased road traffic.

The way in which railway subjects are treated by feature film producers and directors varies, from a crass and insensitive ignorance to an intelligent and sympathetic understanding which ensures a proper exploitation of the dramatic potential.

Jean Renoir's pre-war film of Emile Zola's *La Bête Humaine,* in which Jean Gabin played the part of an engine driver on the Paris—Le Havre line who, by reason of an unhappy affair with a railwayman's wife, played by Simone Simon, becomes finally demented while driving an express, must rank as one of the best and most authentic films ever made of a fictional, specifically railway subject. The whole atmosphere of railway life and work, particularly on the footplate and around the engine sheds, is incredibly well conveyed in unfailingly accurate detail, and the sequences on the footplate, filmed in a most imaginative way, are from any point of view remarkable. Incidentally, the full version of the film includes shots of the engine taking water from troughs on the Paris—Le Havre line, the only line in France which had those facilities. The Czechoslovakian film *Closely Observed Trains,* a much later production, directed by Jiri Menzel, made full use of its rural railway setting and of the humour and pathos associated with railways.

The American film *The Train,* produced in France, with some early scenes directed by Arthur Penn who was later replaced by John Frankenheimer, included some of the most realistic train crashes ever seen on the screen; they were achieved by crashing redundant locomotives and stock supplied by the SNCF and filming the destruction with a number of cameras.

Some British films made good use of the potential of railways, either directly or indirectly. The Ealing film *It Always Rains on Sundays* included some most realistic and dramatic sequences in a shunting yard, and there are many other examples of films in which railways indirectly play an important part, for instance *Brief Encounter*. There were, however, two versions of *Brief Encounter* and the differences between the two versions perfectly illustrate the extremes in the ways in which railways can be regarded by film producers. The original 1946 film, directed by David Lean, with Celia Johnson and Trevor Howard has for long been widely considered as a classic. One of the main reasons for its success was the completely authentic atmosphere of the railway station sequences, filmed at Carnforth. The sandwiches and penny sponge cakes, under a glass dome in the refreshment room, the smoke, the steam, and sounds of the trains were all an inherent part of the pathos of the situation of the two leading characters. The whole of that atmosphere was essential to the story which was firmly of that period. The decision to remake the film and up-date the story to the 1970s would have seemed incredible, but for the fact that such unimaginitive insensitivity is not rare in the film industry. The resulting remake was a disaster from every point of view, from the casting of the delectable Italian Sophia Loren to play the part of the housewife, originally played by the essentially English and wholly believable Celia Johnson, to the choice of a new location, on the electrified Southern Region at Winchester. What possible atmosphere was supposed to be created, in sight or sound, by the occasional comings and goings of multiple-unit electric trains, at a plasticised and sunlit station, is impossible to understand. Anybody who saw the original film and then had the misfortune to see the modern version, must have been amazed that any producer could be so insensitive as not to realise that the steam age railway atmosphere was essential to the story.

When steam locomotives began to disappear, the difficulties of making films which involved steam age railway sequences rapidly increased and by the time that the brilliant director Sidney Lumet started work on the film *Murder on the Orient Express* there were many serious problems to be overcome.

The unimpressive and overhead electrified Sirkeci Station in

Istanbul was completely unsuitable for filming and it was almost impossible to arrange suitable locations and locomotives in Yugoslavia, so a period Istanbul station was reconstructed in SNCF carriage sheds outside Paris and all the exterior scenes of the train were shot in France. The only suitable steam locomotive of the period available in France was 4-6-0 No 230G353, which consequently appeared to haul the Orient Express during the whole of the journey from Istanbul. A historical liberty had to be taken on the part of the journey which is supposedly in Yugoslavia, when a comparatively modern 141R class 2-8-2, the only other locomotive available at the time, arrives to assist the Orient Express when it becomes stuck in a snowdrift which, in an unusually snow-less winter, had to be augmented by a train load of imported snow!

The authentically confined atmosphere of the interior of the Orient Express was maintained by filming inside actual coaches or compartments, or in accurate reproductions constructed from sections of original panelling. In contrast to the realistic interiors of the Orient Express, the studio interiors of the train in the film *Cassandra Crossing* were almost as ridiculous as most of the plot; the restaurant car appeared to have the dimensions of a baronial drawing room and was just as static, as were the Wagons Lits compartments, which resembled luxury apartments in a block of flats.

The French locomotive 230G353 also appears in the film *Julia*, in a number of different locations and has featured in many other films, so that by now it is probably the most frequently filmed locomotive in Europe. Film producers in Britain are fortunate in having so many preserved locomotives and railways available for their use, many more than exist in other countries, although they do not always make best use of them.

Film directors and railways often make uneasy partners; in fact there is only one uneasier combination and that is between film units, ships and the sea, where the possibilities of muddle, misunderstanding and final chaos are even more potentially disastrous.

Little understanding is shown by most film directors of the

technicalities and problems of railway operation, as many professional railwaymen and the operating staff of the KWVR during production of *The Railway Children*, found to their cost. It is, for instance, seldom appreciated that steam locomotives can only operate for a limited time without taking water and when, after repeated warnings that the water level is dangerously low, the engine is eventually uncoupled and moves off to take water, there is usually a hysterical outburst and frantic demands that the railway liason official must 'do something', even if only sack the driver for inefficiency.

Even less do directors realise the difficulties of stopping a train on an exact spot, within inches, for each of many takes, or of making an instantaneous start followed by lightning acceleration without allowing steam and smoke to obscure the action. The many problems faced by railwaymen involved in film making are given scant regard by certain directors who, though occasionally praised by some esoteric critics, earn little respect from those who have to work with them; such directors hold the view that their film is the only thing that matters and the problems of anyone else involved are of absolutely no consequence. Such an attitude is summed up by the famous note on a progress report: 'Shooting then finished for the day because the sun had moved from the position selected for it by the director.'

Such single mindedness can have unfortunate consequences when filming at a railway station which is trying to operate a normal train service. Some years ago, when filming at Manchester Central, the film unit had, through chronic indecision, overrun the time allowed for the use of its special train, which moved resolutely out of the station. A vital scene, in which a group of actors searched for seats before the train left, had not been shot, so, while the camera was set up on the platform, the actors were put into a coach of a handy express, even though it was about due to leave. The station inspector gave forcible and repeated warnings, all of which were recorded but otherwise ignored, that he was going to run the railway properly in spite of the film company and the express promptly left, taking all the actors on a non-stop run to Derby, from where they eventually returned much too late for any more filming that day.

For the 1978 version of *The Lady Vanishes* exterior scenes were filmed in Austria with OBB 2-10-0 No 50.1171 and a train of six coaches. All the railwaymen involved were exceptionally helpful and the driver and firemen, who came with the locomotive from the Graz Köflacher Bahn, calmly accepted even the most extraordinary demands and performed the most complicated and occasionally dangerous manoeuvres to perfection. One particularly hazardous operation, most unlikely to have been given high level management approval, took place at Feistritz im Rosental, a station on the single line between Klagenfurt and Rosenbach. It was necessary for the camera to be on a moving train and for another train to be seen passing in the opposite direction. The camera was set up inside a coach, hauled by a diesel locomotive which moved away on the single line to a position some distance from the station. The 2-10-0 moved the train of six coaches back to the points at the far end of the station loop line, then, with all the brakes hard on, the driver put the engine in full forward gear, opened the regulator wide, whistled and hoped for the best. The diesel and single coach accelerated down the single line towards the station and as the diesel approached the points at the rear end of the loop, the driver of the 2-10-0 at the far end released the brakes and with an almighty roar the engine took off, taking the train through the station on the loop line, at the end of which the points had been hurriedly changed as soon as the diesel had passed over them. This extraordinary operation was repeated three times, mercifully without any disaster!

Any railway enthusiast cinemagoer must have seen examples of almost total ignorance and a general disregard for authenticity in railway matters. For instance, in a sequence involving a railway journey, it was not uncommon for a character to be seen joining a train of GWR coaches which, when it pulled out of the station had mysteriously become a train of LMS coaches, hauled by a Stanier Pacific, accompanied on the sound track by a three-cylinder exhaust beat and the sound of a Southern Railway whistle; during the supposedly continuous journey the train might become the Silver Jubilee, hauled by an

A4 Pacific and it could well arrive at its Scottish destination behind a GWR King, accompanied on the sound track by an LMS whistle. When sound libraries are asked to provide sound tracks of trains it is rare for any details to be given, since it is a widely held opinion that, apart from the obvious differences between steam, diesel and electric, all engines and trains sound the same, even in different countries.

There are occasions when there is an opportunity to spend considerable time, trouble and care in building up an authentic and dramatic sound track for a film, only to have the result swamped by music in the final sound track. In far too many films music is considered to be all important, even though it may destroy a carefully created atmosphere by becoming deliberately obtrusive. It is strange and noticeable that among the visual arts, the cinema is now almost alone in clinging to the convention that music is essential to guide or heighten audience reaction. The theatre has long since abandoned the theory that music is an essential aid to drama, and intrusive background music is refreshingly absent from many of the best television productions.

The work of sound recording for films can be intensely interesting, but it can be equally frustrating. Such frustrations gave strength to my determination to make recordings of such personally interesting and important things as the sounds of railways, as soon as it might be possible. Early in 1953 I bought a small disc recorder and although its performance was somewhat limited, as expected from the experiences of BBC engineers who used similar equipment for location recording during the war, I made some railway recordings on the nationalised GW&GC line. Early results, though better than nothing, mainly increased my admiration for Ludwig Koch who, in seemingly impossible situations, had used disc recorders to make his remarkable birdsong recordings. Blank discs were expensive, the recording time was limited to a maximum of some $4\frac{1}{2}$ minutes, at the then standard speed of 78rpm, and, since close attention had to be given to the cutting of a disc, it was hard to take in any details of passing trains.

Although I had made a start with the disc recorder, tape would obviously be more practical and manageable and as soon as I could afford a tape deck with a reasonably high standard of performance I bought one and built a tape recorder. The results from that first tape recorder seemed reasonable at the time and although the recordings could not be compared with those made on optical equipment then still used for film production, they were certainly better than disc recordings. The increased recording time available on tape was a great asset and it was, for a while, satisfying to be able to run cables into the garden and record the passing trains; such activities were restricted by the cost of tape, most of which was retained, and the results were uncertain because of the unreliable performance of the tape though that was improved quite soon.

One of the most stringent limitations was that the tape recorder, itself large and heavy, was entirely dependent on a mains electricity supply. The only alternative to a mains supply was a converter, driven by a number of large batteries, such as those used for location filming, but available equipment of that kind was impossibly expensive and its total weight and the size of the converter would have made it impractical for personal use.

Yet three tramway enthusiasts, Jack Law, of Decca, Geoffrey Ashwell, and Victor Jones, had meanwhile been more enterprisingly successful in solving the problems of making some personal recordings on location, without using mains. They succeeded in making recordings of London tramcars at various locations between 1950 and 1952. They used the earliest available domestic tape recorder, driven by a battery/mains converter, which they built themselves from government surplus supplies. The cumbersome equipment weighed almost one hundredweight and the tape recorder, running at its maximum speed of $7\frac{1}{2}$ inches/second (ips), could only be operated for a maximum of five minutes at a time for a total of 30 minutes. Using that equipment they made priceless recordings of the last tramcars which ran over a number of routes around London and many of those recordings were later issued on the Argo LP record *London's Last Trams*.

In 1953 there occurred one of the many crises which were all too familiar to everyone in the British film industry when, a few weeks before Christmas, the company for which I worked suddenly went out of business. There was little hope of any further work in film production, for some while at least, so I set up a company with the object of making use of my tape and disc recorder, for recording such things as amateur music festivals and competitions, where permission was usually given for the making of tape recordings of the various performers. From the tape recordings discs were made for any of the performers who could be persuaded to order them. These and similar events kept the recording equipment usefully employed and provided some income.

Few, if any, of the railway recordings which I had made so far were of a sufficiently high standard of quality to be professionally satisfying, but then all had been made purely for personal interest and pleasure, and for some time to come I never even considered that the recordings would ever be issued on disc.

The original sole purpose of the Transacord company was to transcribe tape recordings on to discs and by derivation from transcribe and record, we chose the name Transacord for the company, with no thought whatever of the obvious and later fortuitous connection that the name also had with recordings of trains and transport.

# Chapter 4
# Steam sounds in Britain

The Transacord company was by 1954 more-or-less established as a going concern; it had provided a useful means of livelihood during a lengthy period of unemployment in the film industry, but had left no money or time to spare for such things as railway recordings. Film work would have to be done if and when it was available and meanwhile the company's other work could be kept going if and when time allowed, with occasional assistance from one or other several sound recordists who would welcome some spare time jobs.

In the early summer of 1954 the opportunity came to work again for David Lean on the film *Summer Madness*, with Katherine Hepburn, which was to be made entirely on location in Venice. Sound equipment was to be supplied from France and for the first time in my experience, the sound track was to be recorded on 35mm magnetic film. The script implied that a large number of important atmospheric sound tracks would be needed and to record those in such a place as Venice would obviously be a problem unless some unusually mobile equipment could be used. Eventually it was decided that all of the many non-synchronous sound effects would be recorded on $\frac{1}{4}$ inch tape, using a transportable tape recorder driven by a rotary converter, powered by car batteries.

This equipment, despite the weight and bulk of the converter and batteries, was wonderfully compact and portable compared with anything I had used previously. Admittedly it took some time to set up and the converter had to be carefully watched and controlled to avoid changes in the recorder's speed, but such disadvantages seemed minimal in comparison with the hitherto undreamed of flexibility which now made it possible to record non-synchronous sound effects in practically any location.

The film involved several sequences at Venice, Santa Lucia railway station and on board a train leaving the station. The line was then entirely steam worked, except for an occasional diesel railcar; with permission to go anywhere, there was an ideal opportunity to make varied recordings with which to build up a sound picture of a busy, steam worked, international railway station. A favourite recording position, though not strictly connected with film requirements, was between the station and the causeway on which the line crosses the lagoon to Mestre on the mainland. The climb from the station is quite steep and the Italian drivers, inclined to be flamboyant in any case and well aware that there was a film unit about, produced some monumental wheel slips and similarly spectacular sounds on that climb, especially with heavy international trains like the Simplon-Orient Express, then still a train of some distinction, enviously watched as it left for Trieste, Belgrade, Sofia and Istanbul.

An unfortunate incident severely disrupted filming and some railway operations at one time. A low platform had been built out from the side of the train, to carry the camera, but unfortunately the height of the platform had been misjudged and when the train moved out from the station a number of ground signals were demolished and the camera and crew nearly met the same fate before the train was stopped.

Some nights later, when filming in St Mark's Square, one of the technicians tested the playback loudspeakers in the middle of the night, by reproducing the recordings made at the station; the sounds of trains apparently leaving the centre of Venice created considerable excitement among some astounded Venetians!

Needless to say, many more railway recordings were made than could possibly be used in the film; the producer gave me permission to keep the original tapes, but disappointingly many of those early tapes deteriorated to such an extent that they became unplayable and some others were accidentally erased at the studios when the film was completed.

Despite the later loss of so many irreplaceable recordings the experience of that film location was invaluable, because it proved how much could be done with a tape recorder independent of a mains supply. As soon as possible after returning to England, in the late autumn of 1954, I acquired a small converter, heavy duty batteries and a new tape recorder. Now, at last, there was the means to make railway recordings without relying on mains supplies, though there remained the problems of size and weight, now increased by the converter and batteries. It was one thing to use a mass of equipment on film locations, with assistants, quite another to manhandle it alone and that took up a lot of time. However, during the following months I made recordings with varying success at Aylesbury, Princes Risborough, Cheddington, Tring Cutting and Bletchley and on trains between Princes Risborough, Oxford and Banbury and on the Banbury – Bletchley line. Loading all the equipment on to a train and setting it up for recording was quite an undertaking, which relied heavily on the goodwill of railwaymen. Some lineside locations could not, of course, be reached by train and the whole heavy load was then taken in an uncomplaining 18 year old Ford to the nearest access ble point and carried to the lineside.

It still seemed hardly credible that there was any serious threat to steam locomotives in general, though the older pre-grouping engines were obviously threatened. Apart from the prototype LMS and SR main line diesels, diesel shunters, GWR railcars and some new lightweight diesel trains in the West Riding, steam was supreme. Even the 1955 announcement by Sir Brian Robertson, Chairman of the British Transport Commission, in launching the 'far reaching plan to transform our railways, at a cost of over £1,200 million, into a thoroughly modern and first class service' did not at first seem to be a direct threat to steam power but when more details were published later in the year the intention was quite clear: 'the final abandonment of steam traction in favour of diesel and electric motive power'.

Obviously the recording of steam locomotives had now become a matter of great urgency. Much money had already been spent and it was still necessary for me to earn a living.

In the spring of 1955 I was with the crew which started work on a film involving a location in Spain. The film *Kings Rhapsody* was interesting as it was one of the last in which the flamboyant but likeable Errol Flynn appeared, with Anna Neagle. Even

*Top:* An ex-LMS 0–6–0, WD No 8182, with Royal Engineers crew, at Kinnerley, on the Shropshire & Montgomeryshire Railway in 1944.

*Below:* Caen Railway Station in July 1944, destroyed by prolonged Allied bombardment during the Normandy campaign.

*Top:* LMS Class 5 4–6–0 with train of empty tank wagons, heading north between Elstree Tunnel and Elstree Station in 1946.

*Below:* The pioneer LMS diesel locomotive No 10000 approaches Elstree Station with a down express on the Midland main line in 1947.

more interesting to me was the train journey to Spain and the steam locomotives, varying from antique to modern, to be seen and heard there on the 5ft 6in gauge lines of Spanish National Railways (RENFE). I spent every spare moment at the railway stations in Barcelona, where the sounds of the wild west whistles of engines, hauling trains which included wooden coaches of equally wild west appearance, were alone an incentive to make some recordings. Unfortunately the Ruritanian film script offered no opportunity to include railway sounds in the film and any railway recordings would have to be done on my days off with borrowed equipment.

The camera operator, Austin Dempster, was also a railway enthusiast and wanted to take some photographs. Because the Barcelona stations were too enclosed and dark for photography, we decided to go elsewhere and on our first free Sunday we set off by train to Tarragona, with another enthusiast who helped with the recording equipment. At the junction station of Tarragona there was plenty of activity and the first sight of a huge RENFE Garratt locomotive. The railwaymen were delighted with our interest, fascinated by the tape recorder and generally friendly and helpful. The political police, on the other hand, took a very different attitude when, within a couple of hours, they arrived and made it only too obvious that they strongly disapproved of whatever it was that we were doing. The equipment was hurriedly dismantled and we were escorted to a compartment on the next available train and locked in, with our captors standing guard in the corridor on the journey back to Barcelona. In the police offices at the main station there followed a lengthy interrogation in a strange mixture of languages. Unfortunately the mood of the interrogation was not improved by an immediate understanding of the word Gibraltar which was facetiously offered in exchange for a quick release. We were detained for the night, during which our hotel rooms were searched and news of our detention consequently reached the film unit. Released the following morning, just in time for the day's shooting, we had a cool reception from the producer who had been told by a practical joker that we had been arrested for grossly indecent behaviour. After all, who would believe that anyone would want to record or photograph trains simply for the love of them, an activity which was to lead to several more arrests in the future, in various places and in circumstances which often seemed much less amusing, especially without the presence in the background of a film company which could intervene if need be.

Back in Britain there was time and money to spare for some more railway recordings. So far, all the recordings had been made simply by asking permission from local officials, who were normally friendly and helpful but, quite naturally, were occasionally suspicious of such unfamiliar activities as the use of an impressive array of recording equipment. In any case there were obvious limits to what could be authorised at local level and the Spanish experience could not be disregarded. The next step was to ask for official approval of recording activities and permission to carry them out at more adventurous locations.

At that time the railways were, not unusually, being subjected to attacks by the press and there was a natural suspicion at British Railways headquarters that people asking for unusual facilities might, for instance, be engaged in making recordings simply to provide ammunition for the anti-railway press lobby. For such reasons the initial approach for permission to make recordings of steam locomotives at work in various BR regions was met with some incredulity. Apart from anything else, tape recorders were then still a rarity and recording was a little known activity; the taking of photographs was acceptably understandable and long established, but making recordings was quite another matter, not least because of the amount of equipment involved in such bizarre activities. Because of this the hire of lookout men was, in certain circumstances, considered an essential safeguard. Eventually the purpose of the recordings was accepted as being prompted by genuine enthusiastic interest, and introductions were given to the public relations officers of the various regions, who dealt most sympathetically with requests for permits and facilities and gave generous assistance, which continued over many years, to this day.

With official blessing I could now make a start on the most ambitious programme that was practical for recording the sounds of steam locomotives in the widest possible variety. There were endless disappointments, especially at first, because of the time taken in moving and setting up equipment and failures in the equipment or, more often, shortcomings in the recording tape then available; above all was the need for the right weather. Moreover my plans were also thwarted by the ASLEF strike, which not only directly upset train services, but had a long aftermath in which staff relations were not at their most cordial.

Fortunately it was soon possible, by devious means, to purchase a batch of tape from the USA which was considerably superior in performance and reliability, though far more expensive, than most tapes which were obtainable in Britain. The American tape was kept for the most important recordings, but despite the use of such high quality materials there was still a slight, nagging worry for nobody at that time knew for certain how long recordings on tape would safely survive in storage. There were plenty of theories but none were backed by really long term experience of the extent to which recordings might deteriorate, or even completely fade away, if stored for many years. In practice the main cause of deterioration in stored tape recordings has proved to be due to mechanical shortcomings in some of the materials which were used as a base for the early tapes.

Quite apart from other problems there were many disappointments from faults in technique. You learn from mistakes in recording, just as in photography, but however much is learned you can still make new and undreamed of mistakes. Each new location, item of equipment, or change of circumstances brings scope for more mistakes and they will inevitably be made, no matter how experienced you may consider yourself to be.

All the railway recordings I had made so far were achieved with the same technique as that used for film recording and this proved to be a serious mistake. Recordings for films, with the exception of those intended to form a general background – for example street noises heard inside an office building – are made objectively to obtain the clearest possible sound track of a specific subject, such as an engine whistle. Background sounds are excluded from such recordings as much as possible by using directional microphones in a reasonably close position; if any sound, other than that of the object, becomes too intrusive the recording will be stopped.

The reason for adopting such methods is that film sound tracks are frequently needed only to support specific picture sequences and a recording will be less adaptable if it includes background sounds which may be inappropriate to a picture. A recording of a passing train in which spring birdsong is heard in the background, for example, could not possibly be used as a sound track to accompany a midwinter or night sequence, and a recording of a train starting from a station where a specific announcement is heard in the background would be unsuitable for general use. When a number of suitable sound tracks have been selected, they are finally mixed together in whatever way may be needed to match a film sequence.

For a while the sheer novelty of being able to record trains was enough and there was little time to spare to listen attentively to the results, which proved to be rather lifeless, even boring after a time. The recordings were too short and conveyed nothing of the background of the passing trains, none of the atmosphere of the railway. Many otherwise good recordings I had made had been cut too soon, simply because of another sound in the background, which might actually have given more reality to the recording. It was obvious that the film technique was unsuitable for recordings intended solely for listening to, and unfortunately a number of interesting recordings were spoiled before that lesson was learned.

When, later on, we issued recordings on records, the film method of mixing several tracks was too costly and time consuming to be used. Still later, when it was suggested that the records had a historical documentary value, the mixing of tracks could not be done because it would have called into question the authenticity of the recordings. In fact, although we do much editing for records, we do not normally mix sound tracks except occasionally when there has been an addition of background sounds, recorded at the same time and place as some of the mono recordings which have been processed to produce a stereo impression.

Before the film techniques of recording had been found to be unsatisfactory I spent a long and memorable day in the autumn of 1955 making recordings at old Euston station. All the equipment was mounted on a four-wheeled luggage trolley, which was manoeuvred around the far from spacious platforms and narrow passages of the old station by various friendly porters. I was at Euston for more than 14 hours on that Saturday, recording anything that seemed to be of interest and used miles of tape. Alas, most of it was quite meaningless when played back; it consisted mainly of a jumble of noises. I certainly felt I had learned much from that session. In particular I realised that large confined stations were far from ideal as recording locations; space was too restricted, the general level of sound was too high and at times the background noise made it impossible to pick out any interesting individual sounds, such as trains leaving, especially since the microphones could be placed only a short distance beyond the platform ends. However, a few of the recordings made that day were later issued on a 78rpm record and because of their possible historical interest, some of the recordings were later re-processed for stereo and issued on a *World of Railways* LP, *LMS*.

At about the time when the Euston recordings were made, a friend in the USA sent me a record which he had thought might be doubly interesting to me, because it was said to be a superb recording and the subject was railway trains. The record, a 10 inch LP entitled *Rail Dynamics*, had been recorded on rainy nights along the tracks of the New York Central Railroad. It was produced by Cook Laboratories of Stamford, Connecticut, manufacturers of disc recording equipment and producers of a series of records, *Sounds of our times,* which were described on the sleeve as: authentic originals of sounds which are off the beaten path of records, not studio productions, but made on location in their natural habitat.

*Rail Dynamics,* produced in late 1952, was introduced on the sleeve by: For most of us – for those who live in a place where only the east wind sends the sounds of the railroad reaching out over a foggy night, this record will be a thing of nostalgia, moving within us the strange restlessness of wanderlust. Technically the transient content of steam, rails, trucks and couplings are a challenge to any reproducing system. The acoustic perspective of trains that rush on and into the distance is a new experience, for it is a rare record which brings you the dynamic sound of a dynamic moving object.

The record itself certainly was a brilliant example of location recording, particularly for thàt time; it presented an abstract collection of railway sounds which left me wanting to hear more and with an envious admiration of the technical and artistic achievements which that record represented.

Obviously Cook Laboratories only produced records for a specialised audience, but if they had found it worthwhile to issue a record of *Rail Dynamics* in the USA then, presumably, I thought, there must be a number of people interested in listening to such sounds and just possibly there might be people in Britain who would be interested in hearing some of the recordings which, so far, I had made for my personal interest and amusement. The only way to find out for certain was to issue a record and see what happened.

The LP record was not yet as widely accepted in Britain as it was in America and in any case it would then have been technically difficult and too costly to consider issuing an LP. Even if arrangements could have been made for cutting the master and pressing LP records, there was at that time no hope of equalling the technical qualities of *Rail Dynamics*; 78rpm records, however, were a much more practical proposition. The master record could be cut on the disc recorder which Transacord still had and the record could be processed and pressed by British Homophone Ltd, the custom pressing company which had earlier produced small numbers of record pressings from previous recordings of amateur musicians.

The master tapes were assembled and edited for two 10 inch 78rpm records, with a playing time of about $3\frac{1}{2}$ minutes each side. The first two records were *Birmingham — Leamington,* a rather abstract selection of recordings made at Birmingham, Snow Hill, and Leamington and on board a train travelling between those two stations, and *Freight Trains,* made up from various recordings at the lineside on the GW&GC line, mostly at Princes Risborough.

56

The simple labels were printed by a local firm which specialised in printing such things as cake boxes, and the records were packed in plain brown cartridge paper sleeves into each of which was inserted a duplicated slip which gave brief details of the recordings, in sequence and included an apology for the lack of more precise information. The records were simply a selection of sounds, which I hoped might possibly interest other enthusiasts, chosen from recordings made in 1954 and 1955 when I had never thought it necessary to make more than the briefest comments about what was recorded. Only 99 copies of each record were pressed, for the good reason that purchase tax – a considerable extra expense – was not charged unless 100 or more copies of a record were produced. The tax on the original 99 copies would have to be paid if more copies were made later. When the records had been paid for and delivered from the factory I placed an advertisement in the classified columns of the *Railway Magazine* and *Trains Illustrated* in November 1955 offering 'Gramophone Records of interest to railway enthusiasts, for sale by mail order at 10s 6d each, plus 2s postage and package' (62½p total).

To my enormous surprise and delight orders for the records came in, some people ordered both and by the end of the year a large proportion of the total of 198 records had been sold. An invitation to give an opinion on the records was sent out with each order. By later standards those first records were somewhat crude and certainly lacked presentation, but a surprising number of people were kind enough to write back, often at length, with their opinions; they were generally encouraging and several requests were made for more records, for which a number of interesting subjects were suggested.

This quite unexpectedly enthusiastic response made it seem possible that there might be justification for making more recordings than had been so far envisaged and for issuing some on records, instead of making recordings simply for personal interest, but there were problems. If the recordings were to be taken more seriously they would have to be made over a wider area and in greater quantity if they were to be at all comprehensive. That would take up a lot of my time and would be costly, for the recording equipment and materials had to be paid for and the costs of reaching distant locations had to be considered. Even by the most optimistic calculations it seemed unlikely that record sales could do more than cover production and manufacturing costs and considerable investment would be needed to cover the initial costs of producing records and purchasing stocks.

Such a project could only be financed by earnings from film work, but that involved commitments to long and uncertain hours for weeks at a time and possible absences on location abroad. Without the financial support of film work the new project was untenable, yet more spare time would be needed for making recordings and producing new records, which would have to be issued from time to time at least, in order to gain the benefit of opinions from other enthusiasts as I wanted to know what they considered to be of interest and value. Moreover, copies of records, like prints from photographs, would provide essential evidence to professional railwaymen – the 'artistes' – of my serious attempts to make as full a record of the sounds of the steam age as might be possible during the next few years. The production of records would, however, take yet more time, leaving even less for making new recordings.

Altogether it was a dilemma which seemed to have no easy solution, it was tempting to abandon any ideas of making more records for sale and simply go back to making recordings of personal interest. Yet the possibilities of the larger project, however uncertain it might be, were so interesting and exciting that it seemed weak to abandon it without at least trying to find a workable compromise.

It so happened that a contract with British Lion Studios was now coming up for renewal. The contract, although it gave some security on a yearly basis, was completely binding in a somewhat unilateral way and offered no freedom of choice as to how or where one worked. I made a necessarily quick decision not to renew the contract, but to trust to luck as a freelance, take whatever work might be available, preferably not abroad, and hope that it might be possible to compromise between the necessity of providing finance for Transacord and enough free time, between films and at weekends, for the making of new recordings and records. Some producers and other people in the film industry, whose offers of work, particularly if it involved going abroad, were turned down as gracefully as possible, told me forcefully that I was crazy to refuse such opportunities just for so eccentric a reason as recording steam engines – an echo of the school psychiatrist of earlier years. The film producers were not alone in their opinions which were shared by one of the original directors of Transacord, a solicitor who was by no means interested in railways. He announced that he had no wish to be associated with such nonsensical ideas and had to be bought out of the company.

Such reactions had little effect because by now the idea of making railway recordings had become almost an obsession and would have become even more obsessive if I had then realised how quickly steam locomotives would disappear under BR's policy of rapid modernisation. It was interesting and from the point of view of the scope of the recordings, fortunate, that many other countries, such as France and Germany for example, managed a modern and efficient image although, presumably because it made good economic sense so to do they continued to make use of serviceable and well maintained steam locomotives for some time after BR abandoned them.

1955 ended with a first recording session on the Lickey Incline, during which the weather conditions were appalling, with persistent freezing fog so thick that visibility was down to a few yards and I could see nothing of the hard working engines until they were directly opposite the recorder. Fortunately they passed sufficiently slowly to make identification just possible. At least the fog kept aircraft away and road traffic to a minimum, but as so often in cold conditions the recorder became temperamental and at times refused to function at all, only being persuaded to do so by drastic treatment such as over-running the recorder for minutes on end, to warm it up, then wrapping it in a duffel coat to retain the warmth as long as possible. There were many missed and ruined recordings during those two freezing days spent beside the Lickey Incline. On the first day only two of the several recordings made of 'Big Bertha', the unique 0-10-0 banking engine, were anything like acceptable; on the second day 0-10-0 No 58100 was away for a boiler washout and before it was possible for me to return to the Lickey Incline No 58100 had been withdrawn and had gone for ever.

The leaflet sent out with the first two records stated: 'We have been recording sounds associated with steam locomotives which, though now familiar, may be rarely heard in years to come – provided that there is sufficient interest we shall issue new records from time to time. The records are 10 inch, double sided, pressed in filled Vinylite material and can be played on any type of reproducer at the standard speed of 78rpm.'

The selection of recordings and their editing for new issues of records was carried on during any spare time, especially when the weather was too impossible for recording. Three new records were issued in late January 1956:

*The Class A3 Pacific Locomotive.* 'Recordings of A3s at work in various conditions: on board an express between Aylesbury and Marylebone and heard from the lineside at Aylesbury and in the Chiltern Hills.'

*From London (Euston).* Described as: 'A sound picture of the departure platforms at Euston Station' and made up of some of the few satisfactory recordings made at Euston in the autumn of 1955.

*Venice – Mestre.* This, the first of the foreign records, was made up of some of the surviving recordings made during the 1954 film location.

Again only 99 copies of each of the new records were produced but, helped by reviews in the railway press, the first 99 copies sold encouragingly quickly, except for the unfamiliar 'foreign' record and I had to make a decision as to whether it was worthwhile ordering a further batch of pressings, which would mean that the small profit made on sales would almost disappear in payment of the luxury rate of purchase tax on the initial order and the cost of all further orders would be considerably increased. It was a gamble, especially since it was unthinkable to increase the price of the records at this stage; the A3 and Euston records were re-pressed and the others deleted when the last copies had been sold. Three new records: *The Lickey Incline – passenger trains, The*

*Lickey Incline – freight trains,* and *The King class locomotive* were issued in March 1956. They attracted an increasing amount of interest, helped by further reviews, and their sales just about justified the decision to order additional pressings and pay purchase tax.

No more records were issued for some time as there was so much recording to be done and in fact we abandoned 78rpm records for new issues since by then the 78rpm record was becoming obsolescent as LPs rapidly became more popular. Moreover 78rpm records were relatively expensive when compared with the greater playing time of an LP, which would, in any case, give scope for a more relaxed and effective presentation of the recordings. The factory was now able to process and press 10 inch LP records and although we had no equipment for cutting the master discs, it was possible to have that done elsewhere. Although, to judge from correspondence, it was problematical how many existing customers had LP record players it was decided that any future records would be LPs. The first two 10 inch records, issued in November 1956, were: *The Bulleid Pacific locomotives,* and *The class A4 Pacific locomotives.* The new records, which were sold at 22s 6d each, plus 2s 6d postage and packing (£1.25 total), needed something better than the cartridge paper sleeves in which they were sent from the factory, and the local printers, having already supplied improved record labels, produced some brown card sleeves printed in green with a railway motif at each corner, the title of the record, the name and address of Transacord Ltd, instructions concerning the care of the record and details of equipment on which it should be played. In spite of those instructions several records were returned in a distressed state, after attempts had been made to play them with 78rpm gramophone needles!

The new LP sleeves included a detailed description of everything that was to be heard on the record; there were some suggestions that the records should include a commentary, or some detailed comments, but these I resisted. When, in 1960, the late Roger Wimbush first reviewed some of the records in the *Gramophone* he considered it a courageous decision not to include a commentary, but in fact it seems merely logical. There certainly is a place for commentaries in documentary films or radio programmes, which may need explanation because they will normally be seen or heard once only. A record hopefully will be heard more often and, if it is not, then it has failed and no amount of commentary would resurrect it. The record can only be successful if, simply from sounds, it can create an image in the mind of the listener. It is the job of the extensive sleeve notes to provide essential information and even more important, to set the scene for each recording. With the aid of the sleeve notes each listener can freely use his imagination to form his own mental image from the sounds and at each successive hearing he may fill in the picture in greater detail. Any spoken commentary would surely be an insult to the intelligence of the listener and would certainly become repetitively boring after the first hearing; a linking comment would simply repeat the information given on the record label and sleeve. Technically the introduction of a commentary would pose problems because the level of the objective sounds would have to be artificially adjusted to accommodate the commentary, producing the see-saw effect which is so familiar in some film documentaries, where the level of the sound effects, or background music, is abruptly reduced just before the commentator speaks and increased as soon as he has finished.

Only two Transacord records have included the spoken word with railway sounds. The first was a children's record of *Edward and Gordon* and *Edward's Day Out,* two of the Reverend Awdry's railway stories. The author read the stories which were illustrated by the recorded 'voices' of the engines taking part. The record has long since been deleted, small scale production costs, royalties to the publishers and discounts to retailers having made it impossible to sell the record at a reasonable price. The second and later one was a recorded version of *The Knotty,* a musical documentary produced by Peter Cheeseman at the Victoria Theatre, Stoke on Trent, which, in words, songs and railway sounds, tells the story of the railways and specifically the North Staffordshire Railway, from the earliest days to the 1923 grouping. The record, issued by Argo in 1970, was produced jointly with Kevin Daly, then a Decca engineer, who has since produced many interesting and historically important records and has given much valuable assistance to Transacord.

In earlier years many other people well known in railway enthusiast circles helped Transacord by purchasing records and making suggestions for future recordings. Such support was invaluable, as was the information which was provided concerning locations which might be suitable for recording, and details of the workings of various locomotives.

Looking back at diaries of the time, 1956 was a year of extraordinary activity as far as I was concerned. There was so much to be done and it was a problem to know in what order it should be attempted. Every spare moment was spent in making new recordings and when working on films, a total of three during the year, that spare time was limited to occasional evenings and most weekends, during which some of the more distant locations could only be reached by travelling overnight, after a day's filming on Friday and returning overnight on Saturday, so as to spend Sunday preparing material for new records and attending to record sales and correspondence.

The weather in 1956 was abysmal in contrast to the brilliant summer of 1955, and many recordings were ruined by wind or rain, particularly disappointing after travelling to a distant location. The year began with frost, fog and snow, conditions were less severe in the south and I had permits available for Basingstoke and the line to Salisbury, on which there should be opportunities to record pre-group SR engines and Bulleid Pacifics, which were soon to be rebuilt so drastically that it seemed certain that the individualistic sounds of the original engines might disappear completely. The Bulleid Pacifics were not the only engines whose 'voices' might be changed: the A3 and A4 Pacifics, and the Kings and Castles were soon to be fitted with double chimneys which, as I found from previous experience, made a considerable difference to the sounds, so it was important to record such engines in their original condition while it was still possible.

There were occasional pleasant surprises close to home, such as the brief return of one of the stately and well-proportioned ex-

GC 4-6-2 tank engines on Marylebone-Princes Risborough trains. On a beautiful spring evening, 50 years after Great Central passenger services first ran over the GW&GC line, I recorded Class A5 No 69804 in near perfect conditions, leaving Princes Risborough with a train for Marylebone; as the A5 climbed away, an A3 Pacific, *Prince of Wales,* opened up after a signal check and roared through the station with the down Master Cutler.

More Great Central engines, such as the Director 4-4-0s, were soon recorded on the Manchester Central – Chester Northgate line of the CLC; LMS compound 4-4-0s were also recorded in the Manchester area and between Leeds and Shipley, and by a stroke of luck, an ex NE D20 class 4-4-0, No 62343, was recorded departing from Leeds City with a train for Selby. Hitchin was among my favourite locations for Gresley Pacifics at speed which I visited frequently, as was the north end of Stoke tunnel, where the Pacifics and other engines made a fine sound as they climbed up from Grantham and entered the tunnel, one after another, while in the background an occasional 2-8-0 climbed away on the single line towards Stainby, with iron ore empties from nearby High Dyke Sidings, The only trouble with Stoke summit was that it was plagued by aircraft noise, except at weekends and it was only worth going there on Saturdays when, during that summer, the wind always seemed to be blowing strongly across the track and seldom carried the sounds of the trains climbing up from Grantham.

Grantham I visited many times, especially on summer Saturdays, for it was a splendid place and although traffic noise could be troublesome at the north end of the station, there was an excellent recording position to the south of the station just beyond the up platform. There, shielded by buildings at the rear, there was just space between the sidings to set up the recording equipment and settle down for the day – or part of the night – ideally placed to record the changing of engines and the departure of a procession of trains on the last lap of their journey to Kings Cross. Grantham too had a problem, in the person of a large, officious and no doubt efficient stationmaster who, for reasons of his own, did not seem well disposed to railway enthusiasts, still less to the use of mysterious recording equipment despite my permits, or for that matter engine crews. He customarily stood at the end of the up platform when supervising engine changing; one evening V2 No 60881 backed on to a train and coupled up, the stationmaster stood back as the whistles blew, 60881 started with a slip which even by V2 standards was prodigious, and from a liberally priming chimney drenched the stationmaster with warm and greasily sooty water. It might have been accidental but for the fact that the grinning driver gave a thumbs up sign as the engine passed, and with no hint of a slip climbed away towards Stoke summit; unfortunately the whole performance was so diverting that the recording was completely ruined by inattention.

Tape recording equipment invariably attracted attention and its presence was sometimes mystifying; at Peterborough a shunter in Nene Carriage Sidings was recorded explaining to his mate that the mysterious recording equipment was something used 'to make tests for this 'ere radio activity'. On one occasion, at Retford station, the driver of an A3 made an exceptionally vigorous and slippery start with a southbound express, which would have made an excellent recording but for the fact that a group of his mates stood round the microphone, loudly discussing his performance in terms which it would have been unwise to include on any record.

Retford was a splendid place when, before the underpass was built, the GC Sheffield – Clarborough Junction line crossed the main line on the level at the south end of the station. It was incredible how the signalmen managed to fit in so much traffic, only rarely causing any delay to main line trains. There was considerable through traffic on the GC line and many light engine movements to and from the shed to the east of the station; such engines as GC 2-8-0s, with a surprising alacrity, clanked and clattered over the crossing in the wake of main line expresses, the engines of which usually whistled in a most satisfying way. To add to the variety trains from Sheffield, if calling at Retford, approached the station from the west round a sharp curve and squealed away round an equally sharp curve, to regain the GC line. The worst problem at Retford was a nearby RAF airfield from which at times an almost continuous procession of noisy aircraft made practice sorties over the railway. It was then pointless to attempt any recording, but fortunately the RAF took weekends off and on Saturdays the loudest sounds, apart from the trains, came from excited young train spotters.

The best recording position was on a patch of waste ground opposite Retford Crossing signalbox; the only way to reach it was by humping heavy equipment across the running lines, this had to be done with extreme caution and took some time so once set up it was tempting to stay as long as possible, but it was usually rewarding. The sounds of an express on the East Coast main line, whistling at the approach to the crossing and not always it seemed within the permanent speed limit, clattering rhythmically over the near right angle crossing followed by a clanking 2-8-0 moving smartly across the main line would be unforgettable, even if they could not still be heard on records.

Much further south the Somerset & Dorset line, which I visited briefly during the winter, was an obvious target for recording; on summer Saturdays there was the procession of through trains, out in the morning and back in the afternoon, and on weekdays the double-headed *Pines Express* and the goods trains hauled by the S&D 2-8-0s. I went to Templecombe first, because the then busy station offered opportunities for recording some of the older SR engines and the Bulleid Pacifics speeding through or leaving the station, on the climb towards Milborne Port, in addition to S&D trains. Unfortunately, before I could make recordings of SR workings I had to obtain an additional permit from Waterloo. The stationmaster was an SR man and proud of it; his was an SR station and a permit issued for the S&D line, even though it mentioned Templecombe, only covered the single platform used by S&D trains and did not permit access to any other part of the station or yard for the purpose of recording SR workings. The working of S&D trains at Templecombe was unusually interesting; the station was approached by a steep climb on a curve from the S&D main line proper which passed under the SR line to the east of the station. Trains from Bournemouth towards Bath stopped just beyond

*Top:* On the Italian State Railways (FS) in 1947. An American 2–8–0 at the head of an express for Rome takes water at Civitavecchia station.

*Below:* Filming at Venice station in 1954. Director David Lean second on left, in profile. Author, with headphones and 'portable' recording equipment. *Per Olow*

*Top:* Wrong line working at the bottom of the garden. An up express climbs out from Princes Risborough towards London on the 1 in 88 down line. The 'I Spy' signal box mentioned in the text is on the left.

*Centre:* The author makes a test recording of a Birmingham–Paddington express on the GW&GC line at Princes Risborough. *John Aldred*

*Below:* 0–4–2 tank engine and *Thrush* coach, approaching Princes Risborough with the final auto train from High Wycombe on 17 June 1962.

Templecombe Junction, an engine from Templecombe S&D shed was then attached to the rear of the train and with the original train engine now running tender first, as banker, the train reversed and climbed round the curve into Templecombe station. After station work was complete the cavalcade returned to the junction where the Templecombe engine dropped off at the rear, and the train continued towards Bath, behind the original engine.

The stationmaster at Evercreech Junction, in contrast to the iron-minded potentate of Templecombe, could not have been more interested and helpful. His was a charming station where the spotless waiting room always had a cheerful fire in winter or a vase of fresh flowers in the summer, standing on a highly polished table which also carried a good selection of magazines. It was a busy station where pilot engines, usually LMS or Midland 2P class 4-4-0s, were attached to heavy northbound expresses before they left on the long, steep climb through the Mendips. There was constant activity by 2-8-0s in the large yard and trains came and went on the Highbridge branch line, usually headed by 3F class 0-6-0s but occasionally by a Johnson 0-4-4 tank engine, the first recording of which was ruined by wind and rain. Two further recordings were attempted, both involving a pre-dawn start; one was frustrated by an equipment fault, which developed after arrival at Evercreech, and the other by a message from the stationmaster, on a perfect summer morning, that the engine had been taken out of service at the last moment for urgent attention to the boiler tubes. Sadly, I never managed to record the Johnson tank on the Highbridge branch. Other visits to the S&D, particularly to Windsor Hill tunnel, always seemed to be plagued with bad weather.

I spent several weeks during the summer of 1956 working in the crew filming *Three Men in a Boat;* we spent much of the time huddled on or beside the Thames, waiting for the rain to stop or watching extras in boats spinning helplessly around on, or sometimes in, the river, in gale force winds. On a Saturday free from filming I went to Folkestone, with the intention of recording the boat trains, headed and banked by three or more R1 class 0-6-0 tank engines on the 1 in 30 climb from Folkestone

Harbour to Folkestone Junction. The gales however had not abated and the violent winds which had blown up by mid-morning sent seas crashing over the breakwater and made recording quite impossible; any self-pity I might have had was reduced by watching the unfortunate passengers staggering off the cross channel ferries. Returning the following weekend in slightly better conditions it was possible, after finding a sheltered position, to make two recordings of the R1 tanks as they slogged up the gradient, raising echoes around the town. The speed of change around the BR system was only too apparent here since before it was possible for me to make another attempt in better weather the R1 tanks had been replaced by 0-6-0 pannier tanks from the WR, the sounds of which were of a different vintage from those of the ex SECR engines, though infinitely more interesting than the sounds of the multiple-unit electric boat trains which now whine effortlessly up the gradient.

One of the many helpful suggestions for new recordings had given me some details of banana trains on the Ribble branch which ran from Preston Docks, through a short tunnel and on a final gradient of 1 in 29, under the gantry on which stood No 2A signalbox, entered the yard to the west of Preston station. The yardmaster helpfully suggested that it would be safer if he or one of his inspectors acted as guide and assistant. The Ribble branch trains were worked by LNW 0-8-0s which, starting from the docks, then charged across a level crossing, through the tunnel and a narrow cutting and emerged from beneath the signalbox, coughing and panting to a stop in the yard, usually almost completely winded by the climb. If loads were particularly heavy another 0-8-0 was provided as a banker, although I did not record a banked train. Apart from the banana trains Preston seemed a possible venue for recording various other engines, especially ex L&Y types, but because of the many limited clearances around Preston station it was impossible to find safe and satisfactory recording positions. Thanks to the yardmaster and his inspectors, I made some interesting recordings of L&Y saddle tank No 51423 and other engines, hard at work in Butler Street yard and those and the banana train recordings made the two days at Preston worthwhile.

I made many recordings on board trains hauled by a variety of engines, sometimes simply because there was a reasonable chance of making a successful recording of a vintage engine from a train when weather, or other conditions made it unlikely that a lineside recording would be satisfactory. An especially interesting recording was made one September Saturday in 1956, at the suggestion of Richard Hardy, then Shedmaster at Stewarts Lane, who acted as assistant fireman, on the 11.50am train from Victoria to Ramsgate. The engine, E1 class 4-4-0 No 31019, was in the charge of Sam Gingell, a remarkable driver whose exploits were well known at the time. With a 276 ton gross load and despite signal and permanent way checks, he managed to complete the $35\frac{1}{2}$ mile journey to Chatham in $9\frac{1}{2}$ minutes under schedule. The engine was worked on full regulator with a cut off varying from 60 per cent on the climb to Grosvenor Bridge, to 25 per cent at Farningham Road, passed at 80mph, and 35 per cent on the subsequent climb to Meopham, passed at 60mph. The sounds of the engine, heard from the leading coach, were so loud that it was difficult to restrain the recording level, but, in general, the recording was most successful.

It was occasionally possible to record pre-group engines in unlikely places, far removed from their original lines. Class G5 ex NER 0-4-4 tank engines were recorded with push-pull trains on the Audley End – Saffron Walden – Bartlow line, J15 ex GER 0-6-0s later appeared on Watlington branch goods trains, and one of my only successful recordings of an LBSC Atlantic was made when *Trevose Head* left Bourne End, heading a Sunday special train towards Maidenhead. I recorded one of the elegant Wainwright SECR Class D 4-4-0s on the Midland main line, when No 31577 left Harlington station with a special train, in the darkness of a calm Sunday evening in the autumn of 1956 returning south with an excursion to the SR. I had previously recorded the Wainwright 4-4-0s on the Redhill – Guildford line near Gomshall but seldom successfully, as all were hurriedly made on rare occasions when it had been possible to borrow a recorder and take a considerably extended lunch hour from Shepperton studios. One such occasion had an unfortunate sequel as the time for a recording session was

71

unexpectedly brought forward and a group of musicians sat waiting to be recorded at the studio while a 4-4-0 left Gomshall. The production manager seemed unlikely to be a railway enthusiast, so I had to devise a more plausible reason for the delay.

In some areas steam locomotives, especially the older types, were vanishing at an alarming rate; I had achieved a good deal, but time was now scarce and there had been many disappointments and failures, as a result of which several locomotive types, or workings on certain lines, managed to evade a satisfactory recording as far as I was concerned. I never managed to record the LNER Garratt at work on the Lickey Incline, or anywhere else, and all my attempts to record LMS Garratts proved disappointing at best and more usually disastrous. During days and nights spent beside the line at Chinley, Saxby and in the Erewash Valley, there was almost endless variety in the things which went wrong; the weather would turn foul, the batteries would go flat, or the recorder would suddenly develop a fault. Sometimes an aircraft dived from nowhere or a train passed in the opposite direction, drowning all sounds of an approaching Garratt or when all other conditions were favourable, any Garratts which appeared were certain to be in deplorable condition, shrouded in steam and making most uncharacteristic noises. There seemed to be a jinx on Garratts and it was not until years later, in Spain, that I made any satisfactory recordings of those unusual engines; even then my attempts were dogged by unexpectedly appalling weather or sudden cancellations of scheduled services. Later intentions to record Garratts in South Africa were thwarted by local and national economic crises.

Some other engines also seemed to be affected by malign influences, which dogged many attempts to record T9s, Princess Pacifics, the famous A4 *Mallard,* B17s, Q7s and various ex L&Y engines, among others. Often it was a case of what Derek Cross and Ivo Peters described as the 'You should have been here yesterday' factor, which will be familiar to any photographer, but there were innumerable other reasons. By no means all the earlier recordings were disappointing and some engines, such as the V2s could hardly do wrong; they were a recordist's dream and for sheer variety of sounds had no equal. Their rhythms varied from a steady .–. .–. of an engine in good condition to an uneven .—... overlaid by hammer blow knocks from the motion of an engine overdue for attention; no two V2s sounded the same and even an individual engine could produce rhythms from the exhaust and the motion which were so varied and pronounced that at least one music teacher used recordings of V2s to illustrate rhythmical counterpoint.

Experience with cumbersome equipment used for all the early recordings made it obvious that something more portable would be helpful and at times essential, so in 1956 I obtained one of the recently introduced EMI portable recorders, operated from internally fitted dry batteries. Although I treated it at first with considerable suspicion, because of its comparatively small size, it was a remarkable instrument for that time and proved capable of excellent results. There were disadvantages, one of which was that the maximum possible continuous recording time was little more than 10 minutes, even when using the then recently available LP tape, at the 15ips recording speed necessary for recordings of professional quality. Another drawback was that since the recorder had no erase head each reel of tape had to be erased and carefully checked before use; an assumption that brand new reels of tape could safely be used without checking was rudely shattered when I found new tape used to record a Schools 4-4-0 on the climb from Tonbridge to Tunbridge Wells to be useless, because intermittently superimposed on it were loud tones at various frequencies, which had been recorded by the manufacturers during tests on that batch of tape.

Another problem which showed up in use was a sudden variation in tape speed and a microphonic noise from the valves, which often occurred if the recorder was moved abruptly during a recording. Despite such drawbacks the EMI portable had so many obvious advantages that, once it had proved itself, I relied upon it increasingly and only used the larger equipment for more accessible locations or whenever a longer continuous recording time was necessary. One problem which the EMI portable did not solve was temperamental behaviour, particularly at low temperatures in which it was even more liable than the larger recorders to function only intermittently, if at all. However, the reduced size and weight made it easier to coddle back to life in the warmth of a signalbox or shunters' cabin and then to wrap it up warmly before attempting another outdoor recording. It was not until the remarkable Swiss-made Nagra recorders came into use, some years later, that there was any certainty of results in cold conditions. In January 1966 a Nagra functioned perfectly when used to make lineside recordings in France, more than 3000ft up in the Massif Central, in 3ft of snow, at a temperature of minus 25 degrees Centigrade. If such equipment had been available and affordable ten years earlier I might have saved a considerable number of spoiled and unrepeatable recordings.

I visited many new locations in 1957 and repeated trips to several earlier locations. Despite difficulties caused by stringent petrol rationing brought on by the Suez crisis it was comparatively easy to reach most places by train, given time. The veteran GW 4-4-0 *City of Truro* had been returned to service and in March 1957 was recorded at Ruabon, with a Festiniog Railway Society special train. In May I recorded *City of Truro* again, running light across the elegant but spidery Crumlin Viaduct which was subject to a weight restriction, and then leaving Crumlin High Level station, piloting a 4300 class 2-6-0 with the Ian Allan Daffodil Express. Later the same day, an attempt to record the Daffodil Express leaving Swansea High Street was thwarted by the inopportune appearance of a light engine, which stopped at a nearby signal and drowned all other sounds with an ear-piercing escape of steam from the safety valves.

I spent days beside the line at Dainton and Rattery, plagued by indifferent summer weather and technical difficulties, often caused by damp. Nearer home the Watlington branch line closed to passenger traffic and I had a busy day recording all the trains which ran on Saturday 29 June 1957, the last day of passenger services. I made a totally abortive trip to Shap, where, for three days and nights, high winds and heavy showers made any useful recording impossible, ruining attempted takes of such engines as

74

LNW 0-8-0s and an unassisted 2P 4-4-0, which it was subsequently impossible to repeat. My first recordings were then made in Scotland where, after an overnight journey to Beattock, I lugged the equipment some miles up Beattock bank in a search for a suitable recording position. It was obvious during that first day that incessant noise from the nearby main road was liable to spoil any recording and the two following days I spent around Beattock Station, where recordings were made of various Caledonian, LMS and standard engines. The most memorable sounds were produced by an ex Caledonian 0-6-0 No 57583 which, running on one cylinder at the head of a northbound freight train, limped into the yard. The driver's description of his engine's ailments had, though, to be censored.

Back south again, I recorded the pannier tanks which, with warning bell clanging and attended by a shunter with a red flag, slowly progressed along the quayside at Weymouth with Channel Islands boat trains. Further west I managed to record Adams 4-4-2 tank No 30582, built in 1885, hard at work on the Axminster – Lyme Regis branch line soon to be replaced by more modern locomotives, not entirely successfully, before closure came.

Whenever time could be spared from other activities, we published new records such as *The Dukedogs* at work on the Cambrian line, and Sam Gingell's rousing *Victoria – Chatham* journey; both were issued as 10 inch LPs during 1957.

I had little time to spare for anything other than work of one sort or another, not even for my long suffering family, who were used to hearing trains in real life day and night at the bottom of the garden, and now became equally used to the sounds of trains inside the house at all hours. My wife not only put up with that, but also gave invaluable help with the book-keeping, correspondence and orders for records, which had to be inspected, packed and despatched by post; without her help the whole project would have become impossible.

The records gradually became more sophisticated, as did the record sleeves which were now made from white glazed card and for the first time included a cover picture, many of which were the work of Colin Walker, the prolific photographer and author, who also assisted from time to time with the making of various recordings.

The style of the original recordings also changed gradually; at first, when the main urgency was to record as many as possible of the older engines, recording locations were dictated mainly by the workings and whereabouts of such engines and in any case the earlier recordings had to be restricted to sounds of a reasonably high level, not too distant from the microphones, because of limitations imposed by the equipment. When vintage locomotives had been recorded, or withdrawn, and improved equipment and materials were available, it became possible to be more ambitious and to look for locations where, irrespective of locomotive types, the atmosphere of railways in the steam age might be conveyed by the various sounds of trains in a distinctive setting as was being done in the USA by Winston Link, whose records remain some of the finest ever produced of railway subjects.

Vintage locomotives could occasionally be recorded in atmospheric settings, such as the Abergavenny — Merthyr line on which the SLS ran a special last train headed by two ex LNWR engines, a Webb 0-6-2 coal tank and an 0-8-0, on Sunday 5 January 1958. The superb sounds echoing around the Clydach Valley as the train left Govilon were among those successfully recorded, and at the end of the day the sights and sounds of the two engines storming up the final 1 in 40 from Brecon Road to Abergavenny Junction, whistling shrilly and accompanied by a fusillade of detonators, remain quite unforgettable, though in the bitter cold of that winter night nothing could persuade the equipment to operate properly and the recording of that final arrival proved to be completely useless, when it was played back in an only slightly warmer bedroom at my hotel.

A somewhat abortive trip to Scotland which coincided with deep snow on the West Highland line was brought to a premature end because a film company wanted me to go to Vienna immediately, to work on Anatole Litvak's production *The Journey*. That first trip to Vienna was for a few days only, during which it had to be decided whether the unfamiliar recording system used there would satisfy the requirements of an

American production. The journey, on the Ostend – Vienna Express, was not uneventful. It started well, the train was warm and comfortable, in contrast to the ice and snow outside; a steam locomotive headed the train to Aachen and I saw many others on the earlier part of the journey. Steam became rare as the train ran on, under the wires in Germany, so there was a chance to catch up with much needed sleep. In the early hours of the morning, somewhere beyond Nuremberg, the Ostend–Vienna Express rocked and shuddered to a sudden noisy halt, followed by total silence soon broken by an agitated Wagons Lits attendant and the by now thoroughly awake passengers. One bogie of the electric locomotive had derailed, probably by snow and ice, but fortunately the alert driver had quickly halted the train; the locomotive stayed upright and not even the leading luggage van had been derailed. The train remained isolated in deep snow until, commendably quickly, a steam locomotive came to the rescue; the train was examined and minus the derailed electric locomotive, was hauled back to Nuremberg, from where it resumed its journey a while later, eventually reaching Vienna $6\frac{1}{2}$ hours late.

After three weeks back in England I returned to Vienna, this time via Hook of Holland and Munich, to familiarise the Austrian sound recordists with new American equipment. A month in Austria enabled me to see something of the OBB steam locomotives at work on the long and spectacular climb from Gloggnitz to Semmering. Heavy international trains, sometimes double headed, were invariably assisted by one or more banking engines and a journey made on such a train made Lickey, Shap and Beattock seem tame by comparison. Yet it was noticeable, especially when it was possible for me to borrow some equipment and make a few lineside recordings, that the sounds of the Austrian engines were much less crisp and determined than those of British engines. Before returning to England, I was also able to see, but not record, narrow gauge and Czechoslovakian steam locomotives at Gmund, to which the journey from Vienna was made on the Vindobona, a pre-war Deutsche Reichsbahn vintage diesel express train, with restaurant service, which daily made the 12 hour journey from Vienna to Prague, Dresden and Berlin, with connections which offered a through service between Rome and Copenhagen.

Back home again I had a letter from a BR fireman, R. Scanlon, who had been most helpful when recordings were made of Director class 4-4-0 *Jutland* on the CLC lines in 1956; he enquired if and when any of the recordings would be available on a record and also mentioned that he had been off work during the year following an accident. It emerged that he was the fireman on class 8F 2-8-0 No 48188 which was involved in the tragic collision at Chapel-en-le-Frith on 9 February 1957, in which his driver, John Axon GC and a guard were killed.

No 48188 was at the head of the 11.05am Buxton to Arpley (Warrington) freight train of 650 tons. Near the summit of the steep climb to Bibbington's Sidings the steam brake valve joint blew out and the cab of No 48188 was filled with scalding steam, despite which the crew partly managed to close the regulator. Driver Axon told Fireman Scanlon to jump off and apply as many as possible of the wagon hand brakes, but because of the speed of the train he could not drop more than six or seven brake handles and even then was not able to pin them down. Driver Axon could have saved his life by leaving the engine at the same time, but he stayed on the footplate enveloped in steam and warned the signalman at Dove Holes by whistle signals that the train was out of control. At Chapel-en-le-Frith South the runaway train, travelling at about 55mph, collided with the back of a Rowsley – Edgeley (Stockport) freight train, travelling at 20mph. Driver Axon and the guard of the Rowsley – Edgeley freight train were killed in the collision. Driver John Axon was posthumously awarded the George Cross in recognition of his outstanding devotion to duty, and Fireman R. Scanlon and Guard A. Ball of the Buxton – Arpley freight train were both commended for their part in attempting to stop the runaway train.

The BBC later commissioned Ewan MacColl and Charles Parker to prepare a radio documentary programme on the life and death of John Axon GC, a most moving programme, *The Ballad of John Axon*, which opens and closes with the words:

John Axon was a railwayman, to steam trains born and bred,
He was an engine driver at Edgeley loco shed,
For 40 years he travelled and served the iron way,
He lost his life upon the track one February day.

*The Ballad of John Axon* was subsequently issued on LP record No DA 39, by the Argo Record Company.

Conditions on the footplate of the runaway 8F, with scalding steam filling the cab can hardly be imagined, though my imagination was helped by an incident in the cab of Britannia Pacific *Sir John Moore*, when I was making footplate recordings on the London – Norwich line in 1958. As the engine climbed away from Ipswich, in darkness on the up journey, one of the water gauge glasses blew out and the cab filled with swirling steam before the broken gauge could be shut off.

I had made earlier recordings, in 1956, on the footplate of a Dukedog 4-4-0 in the yard at Aberystwyth (at the instigation of Pat Dalton) and on the footplate of a B12 4-6-0 on the Liverpool Street – Southend line, but the use of large equipment on the footplate was most impractical. The EMI portable recorder solved some of the problems but footplate recording was never easy; it was difficult to control the recorder, which had to be carried to safeguard it from excessive vibration, while at the same time the microphone had to be held in an optimum position, clear of wind and out of the way of the crew. In such circumstances it was usual, as in the case of the London – Norwich – London journey, for the largest proportion of some hours of recording to be rejected as meaningless.

Shortly after I made the Britannia trips I did a recording on the footplate of single chimney A3 Pacific *Tagalie* with a 12 coach, 422 ton express from Kings Cross to Leeds. The driver was Percy Heavens, well known at that time from advertisements as the man who relied on his Ingersoll watch to keep his train on time, which he certainly did on this occasion. I returned from Grantham on the footplate of single chimney A4 Pacific *Dominion of New Zealand* which, manned by Driver Willers and Fireman Veevers, had left Newcastle at 9.55am with a 12 coach train of 430 tons and was due at Grantham at 1.3pm. The train arrived at Grantham 30 minutes late, with a tender full of poor coal which had made it a difficult journey and it remained so. Fireman Veevers slaved away to coax life into the fire while Driver Willers told his engine to 'come along old girl' and opened the regulator for a spirited climb to Stoke Tunnel, followed by a 90mph maximum down the bank in an effort to make up time. There was a rapid recovery after the severe Peterborough slowing, but by the end of the long climb past Hitchin the boiler pressure had dropped to 125 lb and the engine had to be nursed into Kings Cross, 20 minutes late, having regained 10 minutes of lost time on the $105\frac{1}{4}$ mile journey from Grantham, thanks to a conscientious and hard working crew. Later I spent a whole day on the footplate of an N7 0-6-2 tank engine, No 69719, with trains on the Chingford and Enfield lines from Liverpool Street, an interesting contrast to main line work, but hard nevertheless for both engine and crew.

On the footplate of a GWR King 4-6-0 *King Edward VIII* I travelled from Paddington on the nine coach, 325 ton, 9.00am express which had a 2hr 10min schedule for the $110\frac{1}{4}$ mile non-stop journey to Birmingham, Snow Hill. Driver Stan Newton, under the enthusiastic eye of Inspector Jack Hancock, was determined to show what a King could do and pulled into Snow Hill eight minutes early, having made up six minutes lost by pw slowings at Gerrards Cross and Fenny Compton and signal checks at Brill and Snow Hill Tunnel. Unfortunately very little of the recording of that splendid run was satisfactory. The footplate of a King was less spacious and more exposed to wind than those of the LNER engines, or the Britannia; the riding was somewhat rough and it was hard enough, at speed, to maintain a foothold and hang on to the microphone and recorder, let alone control them. On the return journey with *King Edward III* on the 12 coach, 407 ton, 12.00 midday train which called at Leamington, Driver J.Jones gave an almost equally exhilarating performance, leaving Birmingham five minutes late and arriving at Paddington three minutes early. Unfortunately the recorder finally succumbed to the vibration and battering to which it had been subjected, and, since repairs were hardly possible in the circumstances, only intermittent recordings could be made of the latter part of the return journey.

Stereo records of music were coming to the fore by 1958 and trains were ideal subjects for demonstrating the capabilities of stereophonic record players, so it was tempting to consider making stereo recordings. However, the available equipment was larger and more cumbersome than anything I had used so far. The cost seemed out of the question, particularly as the financing of Transacord's operations was a constant problem, despite the frequent assistance given by a bank manager who had a certain liking for steam engines, but work on Jack Clayton's film *Room at the Top* provided the ability to purchase in a transportable stereophonic tape recorder. It then only remained to find out how best to use it. Various films, such as those in Cinemascope, had been produced with multi-channel sound tracks, but knowledge of such techniques was not altogether helpful because they were not the same as those used for twin-track stereophonic recording. Stereo techniques at that time were by no means fully established and advice and experience on methods of recording, particularly on location, were hard to come by, confused and sometimes completely conflicting. The only possible solution was to experiment. Many of the early experiments were failures, but all were interesting, and when successful, were so impressively convincing that the making of stereo recordings immediately became my next aim.

It was some time before a suitable independent power supply unit was available and even then it was a while before I had sufficient confidence in the new stereo equipment to rely on it for important recordings. Moreover the size and weight of the new equipment had moved everything even farther back than square one from a practical point of view, and the time required to set up the equipment was a further drawback. Even after I had made successful stereo recordings I still used mono equipment for some years at locations where accessibility was a problem, or ease and speed of movement essential, and for locations abroad or for recordings on the footplate, where the placing of such an amount of stereo equipment would have left little room for the engine crew.

At the end of April 1959 John Adams and Patrick Whitehouse, always helpful in many ways, mentioned that for one of their

BBC Railway Roundabout films, the ex NBR 4-4-0s *Glen Falloch* and *Glen Loy* would double head the sleeping car trains, which then also included a restaurant car, over the West Highland line to and from Fort William on 8 and 9 May. This seemed an opportunity for stereo recording, not to be missed. The sights and sounds of the double headed train on the West Highland line alone made the journey worthwhile and I recorded it at Ardlui, Bridge of Orchy, Tyndrum and on the horseshoe curve between Bridge of Orchy and Tyndrum. The possibilities of stereo were amply demonstrated at Tyndrum when the sounds of a train at Tyndrum Upper station and another, more distant train at Tyndrum Lower station were recorded simultaneously. For various reasons not all the West Highland line recordings were successful in stereo and some were later issued in the *West Highland Line* LP, in mono only.

The SLS had kindly offered me facilities for recording on board their Jubilee Special which, hauled by A4 Pacific *Sir Nigel Gresley* and driven by SLS member Bill Hoole, was to run between Kings Cross and Doncaster on 23 May 1959. I had not so far attempted stereo recording on a train and the advice of other experienced recordists was that the technical problems might be insoluble, and that the suggested microphone positioning was so unorthodox that it was bound to be wrong. The only thing to do I felt was to trust to luck and try placing the microphones on each side of the train. Even if it was technically incorrect it seemed the most likely way of producing a realistically exciting result. Early on 23 May the whole paraphernalia of stereo equipment was taken to Kings Cross and loaded into the front brake of the eight coach train, the gross weight of which was 295 tons.

It was a memorable journey. On the down run a speed of 82mph was attained on the climb to Stoke summit. Three times during the round trip to Doncaster speeds exceeded 100mph. On the return journey the speed at Stoke summit, after a five mile, 1 in 200 climb, was 75mph, followed by an average speed of 110.8mph from Little Bytham to Essendine. A top speed of 112mph was attained and since the engine was still accelerating when the cut off was brought back, 'there is little doubt' wrote

Cecil J.Allen, 'that a higher speed might have been achieved if it had been permitted.' Almost all of the journey was recorded and the most interesting sections were issued on the stereo LP *The Triumph of an A4 Pacific,* a record described as 'both a recording triumph and a physical thrill' in *The Gramophone* magazine when it was one of their critics' choices for 1963. Reviewing the record for *The Gramophone* in July 1963 Roger Wimbush was kind enough to write:

> This must be one of the most thrilling records ever issued. Anybody who has ever reacted, however slightly, to the romance of railways and to the physical sensation of an express train travelling at high speeds will want this astonishing evocation.

Bill Hoole listened to the whole recording of his journey shortly before he retired and, in his tiny but supremely neat and legible handwriting, wrote for publication on the record sleeve:

> When I heard the recordings I was able to enjoy our journey again and it brought back many memories of other journeys on the line from Kings Cross .... when great satisfaction was derived from making up time lost from some unseemly delay .... All this develops into a wonderful symphony to my ears, which are so tuned to Gresley engines and A4s in particular. This adds to the pleasure of achievement from good team work of Fireman and Driver.

From now on I made recordings in stereo whenever it was possible to overcome the practical problems involved. Old locations such as Hitchin, Bromsgrove, Basingstoke, Grantham, Shap and Ribblehead were revisited, but in many cases it was too late for the vintage sounds of steam. The LNER Pacifics and many GWR engines now had double chimneys and their sounds were altered. Diesels were increasingly numerous and frequently interfered with the sounds of steam. At Templecombe, things had certainly changed; a pannier tank fussed around in the yard, something at which the former 'This is a Southern Railway Station' stationmaster would certainly have winced. Nor would he have been pleased that S&D traffic, particularly freight, was all too apparently being deliberately run down. At Bromsgrove the banking engines were now 0-6-0 pannier tanks and a 9F 2-10-0, so the original Midland atmosphere had largely disappeared.

A chance to record a vintage Midland engine came when Vic

Forster offered facilities for recording on board the RCTS East Midlander No 4 special train which, during much of a Nottingham – Eastleigh – Swindon – Banbury – Nottingham journey, was headed by the then recently restored Midland compound 4-4-0 No 1000. The sounds of No 1000, hard at work between Leicester and Oxford, were later included in the stereo LP *Rhythms of Steam*. Another Midland occasion a few weeks later turned out differently from what had been expected. Arrangements had been made for me to record on the 1.49pm Leeds – Carlisle train, the down Waverley, which was to be headed by a Jubilee 4-6-0 *Newfoundland*, fresh out of the works. Equipment was loaded into the front brake, a word with the crew promised a suitably vociferous run and by the time the train reached Skipton the equipment had been set up. After a brisk run from Skipton *Newfoundland* stormed away from Hellifield and, reassuringly loudly, climbed past Settle and on up the first part of the long drag towards Horton in Ribblesdale; then speed fell alarmingly and when the exhaust grew weaker as the regulator was eased back, it was obvious that *Newfoundland* was in serious trouble. The winded engine eventually dragged the train through Ribblehead Station, over the viaduct and into the loop at Blea Moor, so short of steam that 20 minutes had to be spent there for a blow up, enlivened by a mostly unpublishable exchange of pleasantries between the crew of *Newfoundland* and the driver and fireman of an 8F 2-8-0 which was taking water nearby. A remarkably vigorous run between Blea Moor and Carlisle subsequently made up some of the time lost on the climb of the long drag, the recording of which was later issued on the LP *Newfoundland heads the Waverley*.

By the end of the 1950s the records had become established, and in their extraordinarily efficient and perspicacious way the BBC Record Library had made a standing order for each new record that might be issued. It was as well that the BBC was familiar with the recordings because one enterprising gentleman copied extracts from a number of Transacord records, added his own linking comments adapted from the sleeve notes and offered the resulting tape to the BBC as an original programme of his own making. It was certainly an original idea which by chance

Top left: Transacord 10in LP record cover; No 4650 at Aston Rowant with a Watlington–Princes Risborough train in June 1957. *R. T. Coope*

Top right: Argo Transacord 12in LP record cover of 1965. Photographs by Colin Walker of the LMS Pacific; Paul Riley of the V2 2–6–2 and Derek Cross of the Crab 2–6–0 and Jubilee 4–6–0.

Below: The Midland Compound 4–4–0 No 1000 with the RCTS East Midlander special train at Nottingham Victoria on 11 September 1960. *Colin Walker*

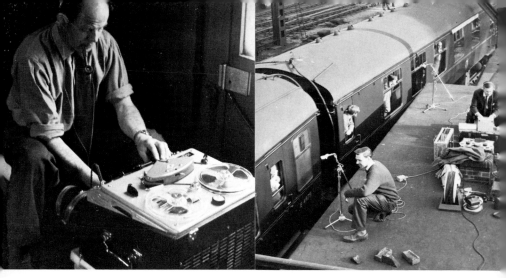

*Top left:* Author with stereo recorder, powered by a battery/ac converter, on board the northbound Aberdeen Flyer on 2 June 1962. *Colin Walker*

*Top right:* David Frost (left) and Arthur Lilley, with Decca stereo equipment, recording the Aberdeen Flyer leaving Kings Cross on 2 June 1962. *Harley Usill*

*Below:* Driver Bill Hoole at work on the footplate of an A4 Pacific. *Colin Walker*

was frustrated when some of the recordings were recognised as having been taken from records of which the library had copies, after suspicions had been aroused by the indifferent way in which the records had been copied on to tape. The records had become more widely known as a result of reviews in the various railway journals including those of societies.

An even wider public became aware of the records when Roger Wimbush reviewed four in *The Gramophone* magazine, in which he wrote:

> Many people believe that engineering has produced nothing more majestic – combining beauty of line with power – than the steam locomotive. Certainly there are few men who are asked every day to perform such feats of physical endurance as those who drive and fire them . . . . . These are the men whose sheer sweat and guts have made an imperishable contribution to Britain's wealth, and who have added a curiously romantic aspect to industrial civilisation. Transacord is doing them proud and bequeathing to our national archives a valuable piece of history. Specialist records they may be, but no Englishman could hear them unmoved – and the Devil take the M1.

Shortly after that review was published the late and greatly missed journalist and author John Gale contacted me and asked if he could write something about the records. We spent some time together, mostly in bitter January weather at the lineside on the Carlisle – Edinburgh Waverley route, or riding in trains or on the footplate over that line. He found the experiences fascinating and wrote a feature article 'The Man the Engines Talk To' published in the *Observer*. That article and a subsequent interview, on location at the lineside near Saunderton, by Alan Whicker for the BBC Tonight programme created so much interest in Britain and abroad that the whole Transacord project was getting completely out of hand.

We had by now issued more than 20 records, including three new 12in LPs, *The West Highland Line*, *Shap*, and *The Somerset and Dorset*. They had been produced, after a considerable amount of trouble, in a new pressing factory and were sold, complete with new and improved sleeves which carried a 7in x 5in cover picture, for 32s each (£1.60) plus postage and packing. The records were still sold by mail order because shops, with the notable exception of a helpful few, could not be bothered with specialised records, and if ever they passed on any orders, expected large discounts and extended credit which were impossible to allow. There were constant problems connected with record manufacture and increasing sums of money were tied up in stocks of records, labels, sleeves, catalogues and packing materials. Much of the money was for purchase tax at the luxury rate charged on records, which had to be paid in advance of actual sales because of the totally unimaginative and inflexible administrators. The inspectors who made frequent visits to ensure that tax was properly paid on everything, insisted that Transacord was merely selling records as a retailer and refused to recognise that the records were also produced, though not actually manufactured by Transacord. An appeal to an MP to be treated as producers and so allowed to pay tax only when records were finally sold had not the slightest effect, probably I suspect because like many MPs, he was more interested in roads than railways.

So much time was now taken up in dealing with record manufacture and sales that I had less and less time to spare for making new recordings, producing new records or to work on films. Film work was still financially necessary to support the railway recordings, and was in any case interesting for its own sake because in the late 1950s and early 1960s, there was a welcome renaissance of British films, inspired by the work of such men as Jack Clayton, Tony Richardson and the Woodfall Company, Karel Reisz, Brian Forbes and Richard Attenborough, and John Schlesinger, all of whom, breaking away from studio traditions and the American influence, made a number of highly individual films which were interesting to work on and were internationally acclaimed.

The running of Transacord had so far been interesting and enjoyable, but I had given little previous thought to how time consumingly complicated things might become when a number of records had been issued. The running of the company had now become a restrictive and worrying chore; there had never been any intention to develop it commercially and there was no inclination to do so now, and a well meaning offer of additional capital was rejected because to accept it, or to employ additional help, would have meant that records would have to be produced under commercial pressure, instead of from personal inclination as and when they seemed worth making. The fact that many of the recordings had proved to be pleasurably interesting to others was intensely satisfying, but it now had to be seriously considered whether the production and sale of records should be abandoned, as soon as possible. In fairness to the many people who had given enthusiastic support, by buying records and showing so much interest in them, adequate notice would have to be given of any cessation of production and the subsequent run down would have to be gradual. Fortunately, coincidentally with a decision to stop producing and selling railway records, a letter arrived from the managing director of the Argo Record Company, Harley Usill, who asked whether Transacord could supply some suitable recordings for the sounds of Toad's train, which was to be heard in the Argo record of *The Wind in the Willows*.

Harley Usill, who had previously worked in the film industry, started the Argo Record Company in Bournemouth in 1951, two years before Transacord began and in exactly the same way by making private recordings and selling them on 78rpm records, in quantities of less than 100 copies to avoid the complications of purchase tax. In November 1951 Argo moved to George Street, London and became a limited company. Operating on a limited budget and with equally limited equipment and facilities, Harley Usill, by careful and intelligent selection of subjects and constant attention to recorded quality, gradually established Argo in a unique position with an unusual catalogue of specialised spoken word, music and documentary records. By 1957 the company was faced with a situation familiar to many small independent companies, that of being unable to carry on without expanding and needing capital yet being unable to expand without the danger of losing some independence. In November 1957 the Argo Record Company became part of the Decca Record Company, but retained a great deal of independence and from an office and studio in a Decca outpost in Fulham Road, continued to be responsible for repertoire and production, though relieved of the worries associated with record manufacture, distribution and sales, all of which were now dealt with by Decca.

I had considered an approach to Argo for advice or assistance previously, but had not pursued the idea; the fortuitous arrival of the letter from Harley Usill now provided an opportunity for a meeting, at which, when the sounds of Toad's train had been satisfactorily dealt with, the problems of making railway records were discussed. Harley Usill was from his own experiences sympathetic and interested; he thought that there might be room in the Argo catalogue for a few railway records and promised to consider the possibilities. Early in 1961 an agreement was drawn up between Argo and Transacord, by which Transacord would cease to manufacture and sell records, the existing stocks would be gradually run down and any future records would be produced for a new Argo Transacord label. Argo, backed by the superb technical resources of Decca, would take over responsibility for the manufacture of records, the printing of labels and sleeves, and the distribution and sales of records. Transacord retained full responsibility for all the original recordings, the choice of subjects for records and the production of master tapes for the records and copy for the record sleeves.

It was an ideal arrangement, which solved many hitherto intractable problems and enabled Transacord to swing into the plastic, internal-combustion free-for-all of the 1960s, with some hope that the sounds of the steam age might, after all, continue to be heard on records, even if they ceased to be a familiar part of everyday life.

# Chapter 5
# Progress with Argo

In November 1961 four LPs and one EP were issued by Argo. Three of the LPs, *The West Highland Line, Shap,* and *Somerset and Dorset,* originally issued independently, were re-processed and pressed by Decca and had improved sleeves. The other LP *West of Exeter* and the EP *Gresley Pacifics* were newly produced for Argo. All other previously-issued Transacord records were withdrawn, but some of the contents were later reissued on EP or LP records in the new series. With the hallmark of respectability given by the Argo label and Decca distribution, Transacord records began to appear in some shops and even at enterprising bookstalls at one or two stations. All the earlier Argo Transacord records were issued in mono only; the first stereo LPs *Trains in the Night* and *Newfoundland heads the Waverley* were issued in September 1962, when Edward Greenfield, reviewing the records in *The Gramophone,* wrote: 'Wonderfully atmospheric as the Transacord mono recordings have always been, the added realism of stereo is a great asset.' *Trains in the Night* was subsequently issued in France, under licence by Erato, and in 1964 was awarded the Grand Prix du Disque by the Académie Charles Cros.

Now that Argo had taken over all the worrying commercial responsibilities, there was more time for recording and for occasional film work. Despite the ever increasing flood of diesels, creating new problems with their raucous noises, there were still many things worth recording. At Princes Risborough diesel multiple-units had taken over most Marylebone local services and on the line from Paddington the smart, but short lived, blue Birmingham Pullman glided past twice daily in each direction, except at weekends or when it broke down and was replaced by a more familiar train, headed by an engine such as *Lyonshall*

*Castle,* revelling in the opportunity to maintain a diesel schedule. The Master Cutler no longer roared down the gradient and away towards Ashendon Junction, a first sign of the political decision to starve the GC line of traffic and reduce it to its final sorry state as a prelude to closure. Kings and Castles, now mostly with double chimneys, still headed the Birmingham trains; until the sad summer Sunday in 1962, when the last push-and-pull train ran from High Wycombe, and a mournful procession of Kings and Castles passed at intervals, running light, into the twilight. The Birmingham expresses were taken over by the Western class diesels with sounds quite unique, which later developed their own personality and had a considerable following when, after a short life in locomotive terms, they in their turn were withdrawn.

Before the diesels took over the Paddington – Birmingham line, I spent some days at Hatton, one of many places which looked perfect on the Ordnance map and the gradient profile but presented unforeseen problems in practice. The most appallingly inappropriate noises came from a metal merchant's yard near Hatton Station, but in a few quiet intervals it was possible to make some recordings of Kings and other engines tackling the climb from Warwick.

I went back to Shap several times, but usually the weather was so bad for days and nights on end that many recordings, especially those in stereo, were completely ruined. Further north and as yet free from any diesels, there was the Waverley route from Carlisle to Edinburgh which was one of the finest lines in Britain for railway recording, despite the climate which vied with that of Shap or the Settle & Carlisle line for unpredictable beastliness. During my first visit to the Waverley route with John Gale in the winter of 1960, the weather was so appalling that very little recording was possible, but footplate trips over the line provided vivid experiences of engines and enginemen hard at work in the best traditions of the steam age. The Waverley route was largely a preserve of the V2s, which seemed to be worked harder there than anywhere else. They needed to be, because that fearsome curving climb from Newcastleton, past Steele Road and out across the moors to Riccarton Junction and Whitrope tunnel, so frequently hung with icicles in winter, was just one of several climbs on that line which made Shap, with its ubiquitous banking engines, seem comparatively easy. Riccarton Junction, with its own Co-op shop on the platform, was accessible only by rail or footpath; my efforts to reach it with heavy stereo equipment were eventually abandoned and when I went there by train, it turned out that Steele Road was a better recording location in any case.

Steele Road was a strange, lonely place; the signalbox was only manned as required, and a porter/signalman roamed around the station with a shot gun, looking guilty when anyone approached unexpectedly. From time to time an old man walked into a field beside the line, uttering loud curses to any passing trains or to nobody in particular and feeding non-existent poultry from a battered and completely empty bucket. It was an eerie place at night when the station and signalbox were closed, and the wind sighed through the Larch trees in a nearby, owl-inhabited plantation, often making a sound like a distant train. I feel certain that the place, like many others where the rails were so ruthlessly torn up, is haunted now by the spirits of the V2s and other engines which, for so many years raised echoes from the surrounding hills as they and their crews passed that way. Even more eerie was Stobs, where the woods above the station were inhabited by legions of rooks, which made some most unnerving noises during the night.

The engines most frequently seen were V2s, but K3s, B1s and J36s also appeared on freight workings and sometimes standard Class 2 2-6-0s or J36s gave banking assistance to freight trains on the climb from Hawick to Whitrope. A3 and A1 Pacifics worked the main passenger trains, including the sleeping car services to and from Edinburgh. There were the occasional A4 Pacifics but unluckily they always passed when working downhill and the one exception, at Steele Road, provided a perfect example of the 'You should have been here yesterday' factor, mentioned earlier. Having recorded the dawn chorus of spring birdsong, which alone would have made the night's work worthwhile, I felt tired and hungry, packed up all the equipment, went off to Hawick in search of some breakfast and was away from Steele Road for some hours, during which time, so the signalman told me, an A4 had finally stalled just beyond the station with a northbound fitted freight. The signalbox was hastily manned and assistance was sent for; a J36 duly arrived and apparently very vociferously, banked the train on the remaining climb to Whitrope. Occasionally a D49 4-4-0 worked local passenger trains from Hawick and I eventually recorded No 62711 *Dumbartonshire* one evening, leaving Steele Road with a Carlisle – Hawick train after a most fortunate unscheduled stop at the station; unluckily the recording was in mono only as the second track of the stereo recorder developed a fault at the vital moment. Luck, good or bad, affects the making of recordings to much the same extent as it influences the taking of photographs. In the introduction to his excellent book *Last Steam Locomotives of Western Germany*, Brian Stephenson wrote: 'I have always maintained that luck plays a far greater part in railway photography than many photographers are prepared to admit, particularly where steam locomotives are concerned.' Certainly the same applies to sound recording.

One of the signalmen at Dent Station caused me a few problems; he was oblivious to the microphones and as trains approached he gave an intermittent commentary on the misdeeds of various drivers and their excessive speeds which, he alleged, had caused the derailment of a down fitted freight train between Settle and Stainforth sidings the previous evening. Recording at Ribblehead was a waste of time during the day, because of noise from the quarry and its traffic. On November evenings spent at Ribblehead Station a near gale force wind blew down from Blea Moor, masking the sounds of trains approaching up the long drag from Settle but carrying back the sounds of their climb across Batty Moss viaduct towards Blea Moor tunnel, so inaccessible that it was only practical to go there with a more portable mono recorder. An excellent recording position at the Blea Moor end of the viaduct could be reached by a rough track across the moor. One November evening the cold, calm weather was ideal for recording and having negotiated the rough track in the twilight, I set up the equipment and made a number of lengthy recordings. When the batteries needed charging it was time to go, but a previously unnoticed mist was rolling thickly up from the valley in the pitch darkness. To negotiate the narrow track in such conditions meant the probability of a broken spring, or getting bogged down, so there was no alternative to settling down for a long, cold and uncomfortable night on the moors, listening to unseen trains slogging up to Ribblehead and over the viaduct and unable to record anything because the batteries were too flat.

Days and nights were spent beside the Central Wales line in all kinds of weather. My favourite locations were in the valley between Knucklas viaduct and Llangunllo tunnel, or between the tunnel and Llangunllo station. One night in the valley, just before midnight, police and farmers appeared from the surrounding darkness, loud with accusations of intended sheep stealing. Explanations about recording trains were not accepted until a previous recording was played back over the headphones; they then left, muttering about various sorts of madness. Later, in March 1964, accompanied by Inspector S.Holding, I made several interesting footplate recordings on the Central Wales line on 5MT and 8F locomotives with passenger and goods trains; it was a splendid experience watching and listening to the hard work entailed in running trains over that difficult route. One of the men involved was Trevor Curtis, an excellent and conscientious driver who had just returned to work after a period of suspension from all duties. His crime? He spent his off duty hours at Paddington, Cardiff and other stations, handing out leaflets to the travelling public, printed at his own expense, warning of the probable consequences of the activities of the anti-railway hatchet men who, by then, were firmly in command in the Marples Beeching years.

One of the most outstanding joint recording operations needing precise organisation was set up to ensure the best possible coverage of a special train, The Aberdeen Flyer, run by the SLS and RCTS on 2 June 1962 when Argo and Decca joined Transacord. The special was to leave Kings Cross at 8.00am, hauled by A4 Pacific *Mallard* on a non-stop run to Edinburgh, where A4 *William Whitelaw* would take over for the rest of the journey to Aberdeen. Leaving Aberdeen at 11.00pm, with some sleeping cars added, LMS Pacific *Princess Elizabeth* was to head the special as far as Carlisle, where another LMS Pacific *Princess Royal* would take over for the journey to Euston. While Transacord, with assistance from Colin Walker and Andrew Raeburn, of Argo, set up two recorders in the train to record the entire journey, Harley Usill and Decca engineers Arthur Lilley, David Frost, and Mike Savage set up a large stereo recorder on the platform at Kings Cross to record the departure. Having done that, they flew in the Decca Navigator plane, plotted the progress of the Aberdeen Flyer, circled over it between Northallerton and Durham, landed at Aberdeen and set up their equipment at the station to record the arrival and later the departure of the train. Unfortunately, much of the result of all this combined effort proved disappointing. The jinx which dogged my recordings of *Mallard* certainly played its part; the recordings of the departure from Kings Cross, both on the train and from the platform, were largely drowned by the inopportune arrival on an adjacent track of a diesel locomotive with engines idling. As for the sounds of *Mallard*, during most of the run to Edinburgh they were extremely restrained, and bore no resemblance to the exuberant performance of *Sir Nigel Gresley*, in Bill Hoole's hands on the SLS Jubilee run three years earlier. On the outward journey the Aberdeen Flyer was slowed almost to a stop by a preceding goods train, lost 24 minutes and arrived late in Edinburgh. On the return journey there were endless problems: single line working, permanent way slowings, stops for water, and delays for electrification work all combined to make the arrival at Euston some hours late. Yet despite the disappointments it was certainly an interesting journey and by no means all the recordings were poor; *William Whitelaw* put in some hard work on the Edinburgh – Aberdeen run and *Princess Elizabeth* made some fine sounds climbing out from Aberdeen and, later, leaving Perth and climbing to Gleneagles as can be heard on the LMS LP record in the *World of Railways* series.

Not long after the outing to Aberdeen, work started on Tony Richardson's film *Tom Jones*, which had nothing to do with railways but, during spare moments on location, gave me a chance to record some Prairie tank engines on the Minehead line. *Tom Jones* took many weeks to make and was followed, almost immediately, by another long film, John Schlesinger's *Billy Liar*. At the end of the bitter winter of 1963, the British railway scene seemed increasingly depressing, by contrast with earlier years. All over the country, steam locomotives were being displaced by diesels and lines were being starved of traffic and closed. We produced several new records but even that interesting job could be most depressing, because it brought the realisation that in the case of all too many lines and locomotives there would now never be another chance to do anything different or better. There were, however, places still worth visiting, such as Gresford, a difficult location but best at night, Talerddig, the Isle of Wight, and the Leicester (West Bridge) – Glenfield line, opened in 1832 as part of the Leicester & Swannington Railway, where goods trains were still worked by ex Midland 2F 0-6-0s in the summer of 1963.

By 1964, the A4 Pacifics were enjoying a magnificent swan song on the Glasgow–Aberdeen line, and V2s with freight trains from Edinburgh, over the Forth and Tay Bridges, to Dundee, all of which I recorded from the footplate. During one V2 trip the large and cheerful fireman had finally had enough of a rather dour inspector and as we ran on to the Tay Bridge a tersely pointed conversation between inspector and fireman was recorded: 'We're on Tay Bridge now.' 'Aye.' 'Well . . . . . . . jump off it will you.' Some sounds from those various footplate journeys may still be heard on the LP *Working on the Footplate,* the cover of which is illustrated with a photograph by Derek Cross, whose acquaintance I made in 1964, after much previous correspondence. When we eventually met, it turned out that we had both been at the lineside between Tebay and Shap on August Bank Holiday Saturday in 1958, though neither of us had seen the other or anybody else there then. In any case, since we are both Englishmen and had not been properly introduced, we would almost certainly have ignored each other if we had met accidentally!

In subsequent years Derek Cross was enormously helpful with suggestions for, and assistance in the making of, numerous recordings in the last strongholds of steam in South West Scotland, as for example a Stanier Black Five 4-6-0 making incredibly slippery efforts to move a coal train from Bargany Sidings, many and various exploits of Ayr loco shed's indefatigable Crab 2-6-0s, the hard working tank engines on the NCB lines and of course, the double-headed boat trains on the fearsome gradients of the Stranraer line. One carefully planned session with the boat trains caused us to spend an unforgettable August night out on the moors, initially at Glenwhilly, where the first drops of rain fell just as the first of the double-headed trains approached from Stranraer, and then at Barrhill, where the trains to Stranraer, lashed by sheets of rain, climbed past almost unheard above the din of a pre-dawn gale.

The Scarborough – Whitby and Whitby – Malton lines were closed in spite of fierce and well-reasoned opposition on 6 March 1965. On that day the SLS ran The Whitby Moors special train over those lines, headed by K4 2-6-0 *The Great Marquess* and K1 2-6-0 No 62005 which, as can be heard on the LP *Trains to Remember,* made some memorable sounds, climbing towards Ravenscar in the morning, just before a snow shower swept in from the sea, and climbing past Goathland in the evening. Fortunately, thanks to the admirable efforts of the North Yorkshire Moors Railway, steam locomotives can still be seen and heard on the climb to Goathland.

The centenary of the Highland Railway was celebrated in August 1965 by the running of a special train composed of the two preserved Caledonian coaches, headed by the vintage Jones Goods 4-6-0, HR No 103, some interesting recordings of which I made at Forres. HR 103 was heard again in the autumn of 1965, in company with GNoS 4-4-0 *Gordon Highlander,* working Branch Line Society special trains on the Dumfries – Lockerbie and Edinburgh – Carstairs lines. These and other beautifully restored engines were a fine sight, in great contrast to some others which were still at work on BR.

Diesels now snarled past with most of the trains at the bottom of the Princes Risborough garden where the *I Spy* signalbox was no longer manned. It all seemed so demoralising. Run down Royal Scots appeared for a while with truncated parcels trains from the GC line, on which the pitiful remnant of traffic was handled by an assortment of filthy engines in various stages of neglect. The GWR engines which passed on freight trains or occasionally as substitutes or train heating aids for diesels, were increasingly uncared for and soon appeared without nameplates, then with numbers scrawled in chalk, in place of lost or stolen numberplates, even without such brass fittings as safety-valve covers. Yet as the 1960s progressed and steam declined on BR, it rose again, supreme and cared for on the blossoming private preservation ventures. As 'last runs' of different BR steam types gathered momentum so too did the following by vast crowds of enthusiasts on the lineside and at stations. Unfortunately it is not possible for microphones to exclude inappropriate and unwelcome surroundings or backgrounds to anything like the same extent as can a camera in expert hands and I did not try to record last rites trips.

I had been extremely fortunate in knowing and having an opportunity to record railways in the time of steam while they were still a living, working entity rather than a matter of curiosity. Now, when the railway scene in Britain had changed so drastically and rapidly it seemed sensible, before it was too late, to pay more attention to railways in various countries abroad where steam locomotives were still working normally on many interesting lines. My final recording of everyday steam on BR in the 1960s was made in November 1967, in company with Inspector P.McHaffie, Driver S.Loveridge and Fireman A.Carr, on the footplate of one of the modern, but all too soon redundant, 9F 2-10-0s, No 92055 with a Carlisle – Hellifield – Wigan freight train. Apart from a visit to Alan Bloom's working steam museum at Bressingham and a half-hearted attempt to record *Flying Scotsman* at Haughley in 1968, I made no more railway recordings in Britain until July 1969, when the Keighley & Worth Valley Railway preservationists suggested the first of many visits to their splendidly preserved line where, as on the other many and varied preserved railways which we are so fortunate to have in this country, it was and still is an intense pleasure to hear again the sounds of steam at work on a railway in Britain.

# Chapter 6
# Recording in Europe – and Asia

As described in earlier chapters I had already made a few recordings on railways abroad on some pretext or other while working on various film locations. Those early efforts, especially the recordings made at Venice SL station, gave an added impetus to the first attempts to record the sounds of railways in Britain.

My first foreign recordings to be attempted alone, and without assistance of some sort from a film company, were made in France in 1959. That expedition, suggested by Richard Hardy who was going to try his hand at firing SNCF locomotives during the pre-Easter weekend, was arranged too hurriedly. Largely because there had been no time to deal with customs formalities or apply for any official SNCF permits, it began fairly disastrously. On arrival at Calais a formidable lady customs official took grave exception to the attempted import of the EMI recorder, microphones, accessories and a large quantity of tape, all described as personal baggage; I managed to convince her eventually, but by then it was too late to catch any connecting trains. After a taxi ride to Boulogne the recorder and other baggage were deposited in a room at a small hotel opposite Tintelleries Station, to which I returned after supper to find the place in darkness and the door locked! No amount of hammering or shouting from an interested and helpful group of people had the slightest effect, so hopes of some late evening recordings were abandoned and I passed an uncomfortably naked night at an adjacent hotel, wondering whether I should ever see the recorder again. The following morning the proprietor of the first hotel explained with profuse apologies that he had gone to bed early, having completely forgotten about his solitary guest and as compensation he provided a free early breakfast, after which I caught the first available train to Caffiers, summit of the long climb from Calais.

At Caffiers the stationmaster passionately insisted that any such extraordinary activities as the recording of trains on the SNCF were entirely forbidden without the support of official documents. The only available official railway document I had was a BR Eastern Region lineside permit, covering such places as Hitchin and Peterborough North and in desperation I produced it. The place names meant nothing to the stationmaster but the words British Railways acted like a charm and apparently convinced him that he was in the presence of a high official from BR; it seemed unnecessary for me to correct that impression and with the freedom of Caffiers station and full and friendly co-operation from all concerned, everything went much more smoothly from then on. I spent an enjoyable and successful day at Caffiers, recording the many boat trains, including the Blue Train headed by Pacific No 231E26 with Richard Hardy on the footplate. The station staff seemed flattered by any attention to their work and were at one time so interested in the recorder that they almost forgot to operate the level crossing barrier for an approaching train.

Without any permits there was little more that I could do in the spring of 1959, apart from recording an interesting journey, which Richard Hardy kindly and hurriedly arranged, from Paris Nord to Aulnoye, on a Paris – Brussels express hauled by one of the streamlined 4-6-4s, No 232S002. It was some while before it was possible for me to return to France, in 1964 and 1965, by this time with the fullest possible co-operation and official permits for the Argentan – Granville and Paris – Rouen – Le Havre lines.

One of the best locations on the Le Havre line proved to be the rural junction of Bréauté – Beuzeville and I spent many days and nights there. The line was busy with heavy goods and passenger traffic and with the exception of autorails on branch line services and one or two diesel shunting engines in the yard, there was not a diesel to be heard or seen. I spent several more days at Rouen (Rive Droite), a station situated between two tunnels and very reminiscent of Nottingham Victoria. At Rouen the noisy work on

101

the preparations for electrification occasionally caused some problems, but much more interesting sounds were made by the Pacifics starting from the station and entering the tunnels, with expresses and rapides to and from Paris, and by the many freight trains headed through the station by American and Canadian built 141R 2-8-2s. The compound Pacifics were not easy engines to record as they had a very light exhaust beat, even when working hard on a rising gradient, but the 141Rs were another matter and could be very vociferous when, as so often happened, they were worked really hard. The sounds of all those engines and the styles of driving were most individualistic and certainly could not be confused with anything heard in Britain.

The magnificent Chapelon 241P 4-8-2s were still responsible for several express passenger trains on the Bourbonnais line to Nevers, Vichy and Clermont Ferrand, which climbs out from the Allier Valley to a summit and tunnel at Randan, where I spent several freezing days in January 1966. The Vichy end of the tunnel was hard to reach and even if a car had been available there would still have been a long and tortuous walk through the snow with heavy and cumbersome equipment. The stationmaster at Randan advised that, since there was ample time before the next express from Vichy, it would be much better to walk through the tunnel and lent me a torch. After walking some minutes into the long, straight tunnel it had become claustrophobically and interminably dark and the target circle of light at the far end seemed as small as ever. Suddenly that circle blacked out and was replaced by two small headlights accompanied by the noise of something fast approaching on the track beside which I was walking, now at a point indicated by rising and falling white guidelines as roughly midway between two refuges. It was needless and senseless to panic, but the torch tangled with the recorder strap, dropped and went out, so it seemed most sensible simply to lie down, just in time as a six-coach diesel express snarled past trailing a cloud of fumes and sooty dust. Luckily the torch had merely switched itself off, but once was enough so I stumbled back to the Randan end of the tunnel, and from high above its mouth made two recordings of 241Ps with Paris – Clermont and Clermont – Paris expresses.

*Top:* A RENFE 241F 4–8–2 emerges from a tunnel near San Felices, with a Bilbao–Zaragoza train in May 1968. *Brian Stephenson*

*Below:* SNCF Pacific No 231E5 passes Boulogne, Poste B, with the Calais Maritime–Paris Nord Flèche d'Or express in July 1964. *Brian Stephenson*

*Top:* A4 Pacifics *Lord Faringdon* and *Sir Nigel Gresley* meet under the road bridge at Peterborough North in the late 1950s. *Colin Walker*

*Centre:* Author, with battery operated stereo equipment, recording a DB Class 50 2–10–0 with a train from Hof, near Neuenmarkt Wirsberg in March 1972. *Brian Stephenson*

*Below:* Filming *The Lady Vanishes* in Southern Austria in 1978. Microphones on the moving engine are linked by radio to recording equipment in foreground. *Keith Hamshere*

Then I returned to Randan station where the stationmaster, having heard the reason for my filthy, dishevelled state, explained that he had not bothered to mention the Grenoble – Bordeaux diesel express because he knew that I was only interested in steam trains! The Paris – Clermont express certainly should have sounded better from the Vichy end of Randan Tunnel, but when it was possible to get there some days later, and by a non subterranean route, the wind was blowing hard from quite the wrong direction for carrying the sounds of trains approaching on the six mile, 1 in 90 climb from Vichy.

I also recorded the 241Ps at St Germain-des-Fosses where I spent several days in winter and summer. It was a busy junction station with endless activity by day and night, friendly interest from all concerned and with the usual exceptions, not a single diesel locomotive involved. True there was little variety in locomotive classes, but that was made up for by the wonderful variety of sounds produced by the individual engines. Opposite and overlooking the station there was an ideally situated little hotel which was incomparably better than some of the many so called hotels which I had used during travels round Britain.

St Germain-des-Fosses was by no means alone in having excellent lodgings so conveniently placed for railway purposes. At Laqueuille, 3000ft up in the Massif Central, there was a small hotel conveniently attached to the station and run by the staff of the buffet, where excellent meals were served to visiting train crews, passengers in transit and the occasional hotel guest. Laqueuille is a junction on the Clermont Ferrand – Ussel line, which runs through beautiful country and abounds in steep gradients. Freight trains and through passenger trains, few in winter but more numerous in summer, were usually handled, sometimes double headed, by 141TA 2-8-2 tank engines, some of which were built in Britain. The 141E 2-8-2s worked between Ussel, Eygurandes-Merlines and Montluçon with freight trains and with the overnight passenger trains to and from Paris. The line between Eygurandes-Merlines and the branch line from Laqueuille to La Bourboule and Le Mont Dore had many excellent recording locations accessible by rail or on foot, and could hardly be faulted from that point of view. Quite unforgettable are the sounds of the 141TAs working flat out on the unbroken 1 in 28½ climb from La Bourboule with the Paris express on a freezing January night in thick snow, or with the Thermal Express and other trains on lazy summer days with cow bells tinkling in the background. Equally unforgettable are the sounds of a 141TA heading the Le Mont Dore portion of the overnight express to Paris up the long, steep gradient to the summit at Eygurande-Merlines station, where it was combined with the Ussel portion, headed by a 141E which took the train on to Montluçon.

I made an interesting journey on the footplate of 141TA468 with the 09.42 weekdays only mixed goods and passenger train from Ussel to Busseau-sur-Creuse, which conveniently waited at Aubusson from 14.33 to 15.05 while the crew left their engine, sat in the train to eat their lunch and then adjourned to the station bar for coffee and cognac. A splendid recording was made on the train for Paris which left Le Mont Dore at 21.00. On a calm full moonlit night the driver decided to work 141TA347 even more flat out than usual up and down the fearsome gradients and round the numerous curves of the line to Laqueuille. The passengers were given rather a rough ride and one or two were apparently dislodged from their couchettes; on arriving at the junction at Laqueuille, where the train reversed, the driver prudently jumped down from the off side of his engine and took refuge in the bar with me, leaving the fireman to deal with the inevitable protests of outraged passengers.

In February 1967, only just in time, I made several recordings on the metre gauge lines of the Reseau Breton, at Guingamp, Carhaix and Rosporden. In more recent years, thanks to the help of M.Rasserie and Dr Claude Bouchaud, I have made many other recordings in France, on preserved lines and of special trains hauled by 141R1187 and 230G353.

The last steam locomotive in commercial service in France was 2-8-0 No 140C38, one of a group of engines built by the North British Locomotive Company in 1917 for service in the first world war. No 140C38 was recorded in July 1975, hard at work with cereal trains on the CFTA line between Chatillon-sur-Seine and Troyes. That engine and others at work in France can still be heard on the LP records *Vive la Vapeur,* and *Vapeur en France,* but another LP, *Paris Express,* is now only available in France, because it is one of a number of foreign records which have unfortunately had to be deleted, since so little interest was shown in them in Britain.

In 1960 another film location in Spain gave me a chance for some more spare time exploration and recordings, this time without any arrests. I made several trips on the jolly little 750mm gauge SFG line which ran from Gerona to San Feliú de Guixols; 0-6-2 tank engines, such as No 2, built by Krauss and Company in 1890, made leisurely progress with mixed trains, which included a daily Correo (mail train) and without allowing for the occasional derailment, the 40 kilometre journey took almost two hours. Louder sounds from larger engines, such as 141F 2-8-2s, were heard at Gerona and on an overnight journey, double headed at times, from Barcelona to Madrid.

In the winter of 1968 I went to Spain again, specifically to record some of the remaining steam workings, fully armed with official permits and in company with John Aldred and his 16mm cine camera. The sight and sounds of a freight train, double-headed by a 141F 2-8-2 and a 181 ton 4-6-2 + 2-6-4 Garratt, climbing towards Fuente la Higuera, or leaving La Parrilla, were certainly some of my most impressive memories of RENFE steam. Several days and nights were spent at La Parrilla, a small but important station because it had several running loops where freight trains, which often had to be divided because of their length, usually stopped before continuing the fierce climb to Fuente la Higuera and La Encina. The stationmaster spent much of his time between trains in his office, lit by an oil lamp where he filled in endless forms and ledgers, most of which appeared to be put straight into store in a small shed that also housed food for the chickens which ran around the station yard. The station staff, who were responsible for individually operating the points from levers by each switch, were friendly and helpful, and on one occasion, quite unasked, went out of their way to do something specially for us. When freight trains stopped in the loop it was usual, because of the climb from the station, for the fireman to spend some time sanding the rails

107

ahead of the train with his shovel. Just out of sight, round a curve, two of the station staff were liberally spreading thick grease on the rails so that, as they later explained, 'the engines will make plenty of noise for you'! That they certainly did; a train double headed by a 462E Garratt and a 240F 4-8-0 made impressive enough sounds when climbing out from that station in any case, and when the piloting Garratt hit the grease the resulting uproar drowned everything that, to judge by the expressions on their faces, the engine crews seemed to be shouting. Sadly that recording and a number of others on that line were spoiled by an unpredictably fierce wind which blew down from the mountains.

After seeking out the 282F 2-8-2 + 2-8-2 Garratts on the line from Lerida to Tarragona, which had greatly changed in the 17 years since my first visit, we moved to Castejón de Ebro where the well-remembered political police pounced once more. This time it was John Aldred who disappeared for a while, but he was soon released after the intervention of a friendly engine driver whose engine had been photographed, and with a thorough if completely uncomprehending scrutiny of the permits. There was much to be seen and heard at Castejón where the station and yard were constantly busy with quite a variety of locomotives, all of them steam, on freight and passenger workings. The hugely magnificent, green, and well kept Confederation 4-8-4s headed the main express trains, some of which made lengthy journeys, such as the 1338 kilometres covered in $29\frac{1}{4}$ hours by train No 5225/135, the express from Barcelona to La Coruña and Vigo; it was most impressive to see and record one of those 4-8-4s making a completely sure footed start and accelerating away into the darkness with that heavy train to La Coruña on a night of torrential rain at Castejón de Ebro. With experiences such as that in mind it must be admitted that although British locomotives were undoubtedly the most aesthetically satisfying in appearance, the sights and sounds of continental engines and railways were generally more impressively dramatic, possibly because the greater distances and the altogether larger scale of operations, particularly with international services, added extra romance to continental railway workings.

The Orient Express was long considered to be one of the most romantic trains in the world and probably inspired more authors than any other train, especially between the years 1900 and 1940. The world famous express first linked the Channel coast and the Bosphorus in 1883 and ran, under various titles and by a number of different routes, until May 1977 when the last through sleeping cars ran on the Direct Orient Express from Paris to Istanbul. Even during the train's final years, stripped of earlier glamorous luxury and most of the restaurant car facilities, it was still an interesting train for a railway enthusiast to travel on, though journalists who made the journey usually described the experience with a noticeable lack of enthusiasm.

In 1954 I had travelled on the Simplon-Orient Express as far as Venice, but that was for a mere 1395 kilometres of the total 3394 kilometres journey from Calais to Istanbul. In 1967 I made the complete journey for the first time on the Direct Orient Express from Paris to Istanbul, and then on the Anatolia Express to Ankara, to work on the Woodfall film *The Charge of the Light Brigade.*

In 1965, thanks to an earlier Woodfall film, I had made the 3569 kilometre journey from Calais to Athens on the Greek portion of the Direct Orient Express, which was divided from the Istanbul portion at Belgrade. During the long journey to and from Athens the train was steam hauled for a while by a 2-10-0 in Greece and by a 2-6-2 in Yugoslavia where several interesting steam locomotives were seen. Unfortunately the Yugoslavian authorities at Skopje, then still suffering the after effects of an earthquake, were not keen to have their engines recorded and insistently confiscated two reels of tape; unsettling experiences like that made the earlier photographic achievements of A. E. Durrant, seen in *The Steam Locomotives of Eastern Europe* (David & Charles 1966), seem even more remarkable. On the 1967 journey to Istanbul the Direct Orient Express was steam hauled by a Yugoslavian Pacific through the wildly beautiful Dragoman Pass to Dimitrovgrad on the Bulgarian border and later by a smart Bulgarian 2-8-2 between Plovdiv and Svilengrad. I made some interesting recordings from the train but, apart from some surreptitious efforts at stations after dark, most of the many and varied engines I saw in Bulgaria had to go unrecorded.

In the early hours of the morning the express was handed over to an Austrian built 0-10-0 of uncertain years, then wheezily proceeded through a corner of Greece at a bumpy jog trot on incredibly short rail lengths. As the first light of dawn took over from the green glow of the dancing fireflies, we eventually reached the Turkish border at Uzunköpru. The Greeks and Turks were not speaking to each other at the time and the change of engines and attachment of a restaurant car were only accomplished after much whistling and buffer bashing. White cheese, rose petal jam, muddy coffee and lemon tea were served in the rather faded brass and mahogany splendour of the vintage restaurant car. Cinders rained on the roof and penetrated cracks round the windows, as an equally vintage 2-8-0 of French ancestry dragged the train up fearsome, curving gradients. Billowing clouds of black smoke indicated the efforts of two firemen, one of whom spent much of his time shovelling coal forward from the top of the swaying tender. The train climbed to a summit on a scorched and barren plateau, called at Çerkezköy, where it was besieged by hordes of yelling children, beggars and merchants, then rattled on down to the Marmara shore at Halkali from where an electric locomotive took over for the last few miles of the journey to Istanbul.

With the hopeful intention of making more recordings on the steam hauled route of the Orient Express and of trains in Turkey, I went again to Istanbul in December 1969, travelling from Hook of Holland to Vienna and then by the Istanbul Express from Vienna to Istanbul. On the outward journey, heavily delayed by ice, which solidly froze train doors, and heavy snowfalls in Austria, Yugoslavia and Bulgaria, the Istanbul Express eventually reached Uzunköpru $1\frac{1}{2}$ days late. The scheduled restaurant car had not turned up during a seven hour wait at Zagreb, consequently no food was available on the train for three days, and news that a restaurant car should be attached at Uzunköpru was most welcome. The Turkish restaurant car was a luggage van, at one end of which there was an ancient kitchen range, fired from a heap of coal in the corner and

110

presided over by a cheerful fellow in a flat cap and greasy striped apron. He did the cooking, served the dubious results to customers at insecure trestle tables, stacked dirty crockery in buckets, spat frequently and fairly accurately on to the coal heap, and collected the money. He was also a saviour to a number of hungry passengers. The heavy train lost more time on the journey to Halkali, and as no electric locomotives were available there an ancient 0-10-0 took over the Istanbul Express which finally groaned to a halt in Sirkeçi station 41 hours and 27 minutes late.

From previous experiences in Turkey nothing that happened during the next two weeks should have surprised me, though this was the first time that I had direct contact with the often corrupt bureaucracy, which it is difficult to overcome. The Turkish railways would be hard to beat for monumental inefficiency and the news that in four weeks at the end of 1978 there were five serious accidents, including a spectacular head-on collision on the Istanbul – Ankara main line, was not at all surprising.

Permits had been promised for collection at Istanbul, but at the end of another wasted day there seemed no hope of getting them so I accepted a letter of introduction with the assurance that it would be most influential and altogether better. Unfortunately that letter had little influence on local bureaucrats in distant places and even less on policemen who could not read, one of whom I encountered on Boxing Day, which meant nothing in Muslim Turkey, at a desolate and snowbound junction station at Ulukisla. The Istanbul – Baghdad Taurus Express had deposited me there, $4\frac{3}{4}$ hours late after a 15 hour, 1121km journey; there were no other passengers, only a woman with no legs, covered in sacking and perched on a wooden trolley on which she propelled herself by her stumped arms alongside the train with loud demands for money. The station staff were surly, unhelpful and suspicious, but did nothing to prevent me setting up equipment to record an LMS class 8F 2-8-0, (a number of which arrived in this part of the world by courtesy of the War Department) incongruously fitted with an air brake pump, which was waiting at the head of a freight train. Before the train left a fully armed military

111

policeman appeared and unmistakeably indicated that whatever I was doing must cease immediately. He then summoned a dilapidated taxi, took me and the equipment to the local police station and pushed me inside, after I had paid the taxi driver. The letter of introduction was endlessly scrutinised and discussed, tea was served and there was much telephoning. 'British' they said, many times as they inspected my passport; then a man in a flat cap came in: 'Speak English' he said, frowned over his dictionary and added: 'Tomorrow – most sorry'. Quite what would happen tomorrow was not clear but, whoever he was, he certainly had good reason to be most sorry about the cold, dirty and barely furnished room in which I spent a worried night. The next morning an army officer arrived; he explained in Americanised English that this was a military area, railways were military matters, I must not interfere with them and must go away at once. I could hardly wait and was delighted to pay for another taxi, with armed escort to the station where the escort made sure that I left on the mail train to Adana which soon arrived, apparently some hours early but in fact extremely late, because it should have arrived on the afternoon of the previous day!

The journey over the 4800ft summit and down through the Taurus mountains was simply magnifcent and more than made up for the irritations of previous days. Progress behind a three cylinder 2-10-0 was slow, the train stopped at every station and sometimes between them, for totally inexplicable reasons which had nothing to do with signals of which there were none.

At Adana nobody was interested in letters of introduction or much else; it's much more interesting further on they said and well it might have been, but I had already been warned not to go anywhere near the Syrian border and decided it would be wiser to go back to Yenice. There the stationmaster understood and spoke some German and was most helpful. His station was busy by Turkish standards; a Nohab 2-6-0 fussed up and down, sometimes just for my benefit and there were occasional passenger and mixed trains on the Mersin line headed by 4-8-0s, and on the main line, headed usually by three cylinder 2-10-0s of one type of another. Northbound freight trains took on another

2-10-0 as pilot or banker for the long climb over the Taurus mountains which gleamed in the background. Around the station, wherever engines cleaned their fires old women picked among the cinders and filled their baskets with anything combustible. Inquisitive and acquisitive children swarmed across the tracks whenever there was something strange to see or possibly steal; they formed a staring circle round the microphones and recorder, giggling, coughing and spitting. Closely surrounded by such disconcerting noises it was difficult to record anything, except when the railwaymen succeeded in their endless fierce efforts to chase the children away.

From Yenice I travelled up into the snow covered mountains on the morning mail train. During the journey the engine slipped to a standstill inside one of the several tunnels, ran out of steam and we had to wait a while for a blow up. The subsequent uproar among the suffocating passengers almost drowned the sounds of the engine as it struggled out of the tunnel and then climbed slowly towards Belemedik, an isolated, primitive village more than 4000ft up in the Taurus mountains and only accessible over rough tracks by donkey or by the railway, which here runs out from the last tunnel on the climb from Yenice and enters a wide valley surrounded by sheer mountain peaks. I spent two days and a night at Belemedik.

When the time came to leave Turkey after that second visit, it seemed disappointing that after travelling so far to and around the country and spending so long there, I had made comparatively few recordings. Yet because the recorded sounds are so uniquely interesting and the whole experience is so vividly memorable, looking back it now seems well worthwhile.

There were plenty of steam locomotives still at work in various Eastern European countries, but several photographers had run into trouble there, even though they had permits, and it seemed stupid to risk even worse problems than those met in Turkey by attempting to record in Communist countries without permission. Unfortunately the mere idea that anybody might have an innocent wish to record railway sounds was treated with even more incredulous suspicion than it had aroused elsewhere in the 1950s. Applications to the representatives of such countries as Bulgaria, Czechoslovakia, Hungary and Russia were generally either ignored as facetious or were passed from one prevaricating official to another and finally refused. In some cases it would have been possible to go with an organised party and accept all the restrictions which that implied; alternatively some unobtrusive recordings might have been made with a small recorder and concealed microphones but, as I already knew, that was hard to do without looking suspiciously guilty and anyway such methods usually produced indifferent results, especially in stereo.

A fanatically dedicated Yugoslavian enthusiast who had managed to get some Transacord records, wrote to Argo at the address on the record sleeves and suggested that recordings be made in Yugoslavia. He added that he would arrange for permission and act as an escort if I would meet him in Ljubljana in November 1970. Quite how he organised everything I never managed to discover, but he certainly prevented any unpleasant international incidents during my three-week stay in Yugoslavia. He mentioned places where we must not record and at times told me to keep quiet, look innocent and show no interest whatever in railways. The greatest problem was the weather, often so bad that for precious days and nights it was impossible to do anything other than try to get warm and dry, while feeling sorry for the Yugoslavian shunters and pointsmen, who were certainly neither as they wandered around under the incongruously inadequate protection of city type black umbrellas.

A single line from Ljubljana climbs along the far side of a broad valley at Skofljica, swings round a wide horseshoe curve and climbs even more steeply along the near side of the valley, through a rock cutting and into a tunnel. That was a near perfect location for recording, especially in the twilight of a calm evening of sullen sky and freezing drizzle when, for nearly 15 minutes, from a position near the tunnel mouth, we listened to and recorded a 1920s vintage, Austrian-built 2-8-0 slipping and struggling round the valley and into the tunnel at the head of a heavy freight train.

In the Istrian Mountains we recorded a pair of Austrian-built 0-10-0s, both more than 50 years old, fiercely attacking the long climb from Rakitovec to Zazid with a double headed freight train. Both engines were working flat out and their exhaust beats merged in a continuous roar at the start of the climb, then gradually slowed and separated as the two engines headed the train away across the barren mountains in the face of a howling gale. Later that evening, down at Rakitovec station, I was surprised to be spoken to in strongly Scottish accented English by a Yugoslavian railwayman; he had been conscripted into Mussolini's army, fought in the Western Desert, was taken prisoner and sent to a prisoner of war camp in Scotland. By the time he went home to Istria, which was Italian territory from 1920 to 1947, it had become part of Slovenian Yugoslavia.

On a frosty evening in the Julian Alps a 53 year old Prussian-built three cylinder 2-10-0, at the head of a 750 tonne freight train, raised remarkable echoes from the 6000ft peaks of the surrounding mountains during the long, steep and slippery climb up the valley to Bojhinska Bistrica. Earlier we had spent two miserably inactive days at that normally delightful place in continuous torrential rain, as a result of which a deep and fast flowing river ran out of the mouth of the single line tunnel. In such conditions the continued running of trains through the tunnel seemed somewhat hazardous, but the stationmaster said that the flooding was quite usual and was no problem because the track was laid on specially large and heavy ballast! He did admit though, that there were problems when the water level was high enough to reach the engine ash pans. A journey through that flooded tunnel on the evening passenger train, headed by a 52 year old Hungarian built 2-6-2 tank engine, was most interesting. From the open platform of the leading coach we could see the considerable wash created by the engine as it plunged ahead at a slow walking pace through deep water, with the firemen leaning far out to keep an eye on the water level, then gradually accelerated through shallower water at the approach to the summit. The recording I made on that amphibious train sounds nothing like a railway journey, more like a trip through a fairground tunnel of love on some weird little steamship!

The eminent Austrian locomotive engineer Doctor Adolph Giesl-Gieslingen, an enthusiastic listener to Transacord records, told me in 1969 that there were many interesting steam locomotives still at work in Romania, including some impressive 2-8-4s for which he played a considerable part in the design. When 2-8-4s of the same type were first built, as the 214 series in Austria, they were the most powerful locomotives in Europe. In 1963 the class was chosen for the working of heavy express passenger trains on mountain lines in Romania and 79 engines of the class were built there between 1937 and 1940.

The first approach to the Romanians in 1969 met the response I expected from previous dealings with Communist countries – suspicion, prevarication and eventual silence. Early in 1971 Doctor Giesl-Gieslingen asked if there had been any progress with the Romanians and when told of the impasse, kindly wrote yet another letter to the CFR in Bucharest. In the summer, after months of continued and absolute silence, a three page telegram arrived from the Romanian Transport Ministry which gave the conditions on which a three week visit would be permitted. The main condition was that £400 in Sterling must be paid in Bucharest for such facilities as the services of a French speaking railway official who would act as an escort; his living expenses would have to be paid in addition, but basic rail transport was covered by the facilities payment. By 1971 currency standards £400 was a lot of money to gamble on a project which seemed nebulous, mainly because specific questions about what would be permitted had been completely ignored. Because of the uncertainty about permits, Paul Wilson, a railway enthusiast and well-known film cameraman who was keen to go with me to photograph and film steam engines anywhere, rightly decided not to go to Romania; his decision proved wise because the restrictions on filming were so numerous and severe that his visit would have been wasted.

Many more telegrams and letters came and went before, in October 1971, I left Paris on the Orient Express for Bucharest. At Hegyeshalom on the Hungarian border and at Curtici on the Romanian border the various customs officials were sternly unimpressed by letters in English from the Romanian Transport Ministry and conferred over essays which they wrote in my passport before, reluctantly, allowing me to travel on to

Bucharest with a considerable amount of stereo recording equipment. From Bucharest North station two officials escorted me to various ministries where, after handing over £400, I was photographed passport fashion by a lady with an ancient plate camera and endlessly interrogated to find out, yet again, what I wished to do and why. My escort, who appeared the next day, was a French speaking locomotive engineer aptly named Gabriel. He was most knowledgeable on railway matters and though no doubt a reliable Party member, had a considerable sense of humour. One idiosyncracy, most evident in the sleeping car compartments and primitive accommodation which we shared, was that he never brought a change of socks, even when away for a week or more.

After two days of investigation, documentation and waiting around we left Bucharest on the overnight train to Subcetate, then travelled by a mixed train headed by an immaculate, Austrian-built, 2-8-2 rack and adhesion tank engine, which later made some most unusual sounds when it propelled the train on the rack section that takes the line over the 3000ft summit at Portile de Fier on the northern slopes of the Transylvanian Alps.

The magnificent 2-8-4s, which had an extraordinarily staccato exhaust beat, had few remaining duties but were successfully recorded when heading express trains near Oradea a busy junction where many interesting locomotive workings were seen and heard. Two of the few remaining, once famous, Maffei Pacifics were later recorded at Medgidia and Badadag on the line to Tulcea, a strange place on the estuary of the Danube, opposite Russia. One of the Pacifics worked the morning *Persoane* (stopping) passenger train, calling at all stations on the $4\frac{3}{4}$ hour, 179km journey to Tulcea and then, after a $2\frac{1}{2}$ hour stop over, worked a similar train back to Constanta; 144km of the journey was over a steeply undulating single line on which some hard work was called for from the engine and crew. The same crew worked the outward and return journeys, leaving Constanta at 08.00 and arriving back there at 19.45. Such long hours appeared to be normal for engine and train crews; freight train guards must have found the hours endless, especially on a winter night, for they rode on the end of the last wagon in a small unheated cabin something like an upright coffin with portholes and not much larger. One bitterly cold day I asked the guard of a waiting freight train how he coped with the bumpy discomfort: 'It can be very hard', he said, interpreted by Gabriel, 'but it is part of railway life and I am a railwayman'.

One of several minor Balkan dramas took place at Alba Iulia, where I recorded narrow gauge locomotives with splendid whistles at work on the line to Zlatna. We arrived on a main line train in the morning and met the stationmaster. At first he seemed suspicious but then charmingly suggested that, as we intended to walk some way down the narrow gauge line, anything not needed could be left in his office. When we returned to the station in the afternoon there were some police and soldiers there; two of each were in the office where my luggage had been searched and it was evident that at the suggestion of the stationmaster we were to be taken away. Tension eased after several lengthy phone calls presumably to Bucharest, and after some grudging apologies we left on an evening train to Teius. My escorting angel Gabriel seemed unsurprised by the incident and cheerfully explained: 'In Romania we have very many important officials, such as stationmasters and some of them like to be much more important than they really are'. That humorously cynical attitude to Marxist officialdom was often evident; sometimes, bored with standing around at the lineside, he would wander off for an hour or so after giving me his black leather coat. 'Wear that, say nothing to anybody and look grim', he said, 'then everybody will think you are one of the secret police and leave you completely alone'. It certainly worked, but that was not the only identity I assumed under his guardianship.

When we arrived at Teius it seemed odd that we walked away from the station and stumbled along the track in the dark with heavy baggage, but all questions went unanswered. We reached a barrack like building and stopped outside. 'Don't speak to me and if anyone speaks to you don't answer', whispered Gabriel. Inside he wrote something in a book, collected keys from a caretaker, took me upstairs and opened the door of a cell-like but clean room, furnished with wash basin, chair and duvet covered bed, under which was a pair of brown felt bedroom slippers. He told me to lock the door and left me puzzled and slightly worried. A short while later he quietly called me outside and we walked down to the town to have an excellent supper in a drably furnished people's restaurant, where we were entertained by a state employed trio of an accordion player, pianist and violinist, who played to a strictly observed state musician's union timetable, but seemed to enjoy their work. During the evening Gabriel explained the earlier mysteries. We were staying in a railway staff transit hostel into which he had booked me as a locomotive inspector from Timisoara under the name of Petra Toma, the Romanian version of my Christian names. 'They make a good Romanian name', he said, 'but if somebody heard us speaking French they might be suspicious and that could be quite bad, especially for me.' I remained prudently mute until we were on the train to Cluj next morning.

Back in Bucharest I was taken to lunch at a large hotel where, in one corner of the dining room, a group of smartly dressed people seemed to get unusually attentive service. I asked if they were tourists and was told by one of my hosts that they were all Romanian but were important members of the Communist party. In the hotel lobby I was taken aside by another of my hosts, an important railway officer, who asked me to buy him some American cigarettes from the tourist shop which only accepted foreign currency. 'Our country is now a worker's republic', he said, 'so such things are not for us.'

The undercurrent of suspicion, repression and fear in Romania and other Eastern bloc countries was depressingly similar to that I experienced towards the end of the war in Germany and must be inseparable from any totalitarian regime, whether it be Fascist or Communist. It is surprising that so much individuality was allowed among engine drivers in some Communist countries; maybe it had something to do with the elite mystique which used to go with the job. In Romania, where the one-engine/one-driver principle was still widely applied, such individuality was evidenced by engines with connecting rods, wheel spokes, number plates and the like painted in assorted bright colours; even the engine whistles were often changed over to suit the personal preferences of a driver. My main regret was that my visit could not be made earlier, but nevertheless my railway tour of Romania was certainly worthwhile. Despite the influx of diesels and the progress of electrification it was exceptional to see a steam locomotive which was not carefully cleaned and well maintained. A variety of steam locomotives was still hard at work in several parts of the country, much of which is unusually beautiful, and it was interesting to see things which tourists do not see and to be so closely involved with Romanian railways and railwaymen. Those railwaymen, working in the type of society advocated by left wing militants in Western Europe, certainly do not have the freedom to disrupt public services whenever they have a grievance.

West Germany was much too efficient a country to provide any untoward excitements and the only Balkan type incident there occurred one January evening on the East German border, at Hönebach, where the West German border patrol appeared in the twilight to enquire why I was apparently operating a clandestine radio transmitter. They were most polite but obviously found it hard to understand why, on a freezing evening, a lone Englishman should be waiting beside the snow covered line to record the sounds of an East German Pacific locomotive, climbing from Gerstungen with a heavy express train, heading it over the all too obvious border and whistling mournfully away into the distant tunnel.

The many visits I made to West Germany, whenever there was time to spare in the years between 1969 and 1973, were a much needed tonic. The lack of excitement in the country was compensated for by the sounds and sights of powerful steam locomotives working heavy trains in normal service in widely varied locations. It was not easy to find good recording locations and military aircraft were a widespread problem. Brian Stephenson was endlessly helpful with accurate and detailed information concerning locomotives and their whereabouts. In 1972 we eventually managed to visit the Schwäbisch Hall and Neuenmarkt Wirsberg areas together, an interesting trip which produced some worthwhile results, one of which can be heard on the LP *Steam in all Directions*. Like several other LPs, this is illustrated by one of Brian Stephenson's excellent pictures.

I made more recordings in West Germany than in any other country, except Britain, and some are particularly memorable, such as the vintage 38 class 4-6-0s at work in the beautiful forested country around Horb and Sigmaringen, the 03 Pacifics on the Ulm – Friedrichshafen line, East German Pacifics on the line from Bebra, the 01 Pacifics on the 8km, 1 in 40 climb of the Schiefe Ebene, and the three-cylinder 012 Pacifics and the 2-8-2s, sometimes in tandem, on the Rheine – Emden line. At Hirzenhain, where a gradient board indicated 1 in 17, the powerful 94 class 0-10-0 tank engines climbed steadily towards the summit with passenger trains from Dillenburg. In the vine-covered Moselle Valley an endless procession of equally endless freight trains climbed out from Bullay, day and night, headed by three-cylinder or two-cylinder 2-10-0s, usually assisted by a diesel banker, and at Altenbeken some exceptionally hard working 2-10-0s filled the wide valley with their sounds for many minutes on end as they climbed towards the splendid viaduct with heavy freight trains. All too soon steam working declined in West Germany and finally ceased, but sounds such as the haunting low pitched whistles echoing across a valley will not be forgotten.

In the autumn of 1973 there were still steam locomotives at work on some regular services in Italy. There, in the Dolomites, the curious looking Crosti boilered 2-8-0s made some equally curious but impressively energetic sounds as they fiercely attacked the steep gradients on the Fortezza – San Candido line with freight and passenger trains. Sometimes some heavy passenger trains to and from Germany were banked or double headed, or both, by two or three 2-8-0s, but so far as I was concerned such trains only ran *possibile domani* and never actually appeared. The Crosti 2-8-0s also worked freight trains on the Alessandria – Alba line; at one station on that line, Santa Stefano Belbo, the crew of a 2-8-0 were so delighted to have their engine recorded that despite the exhortations of the stationmaster, they refused to move their train on until they had heard the recording and been photographed with the train crew and station staff all grouped around their engine. The more conventional and elegant 640 class 2-6-0s were recorded at work with passenger trains in various places on the Alessandria – Alba line and in the Po Valley. A 2-6-0 of the same class sometimes assisted freight trains on the long, steep climb out of Trento on the line to Primolano. At Villazzano, high above Trento, there was a likely looking recording location near a seldom used level crossing; unfortunately, as soon as the crossing closed, a local lady hung her large carpet over the lowered barrier and then beat it so loudly that the noise completely ruined the recording of a banked freight train climbing out from Trento.

Through Primolano and Bassano del Grappa I travelled to Venice at the end of the line. There, in 1973, electric locomotives glided efficiently, but impersonally, out from the station and away over the causeway to Mestre. It was all very different to the well-remembered scene in 1954 when, in a way, Transacord records began here with the inspiration given by the recordings made on a tape recorder which, cumbersome though it was, did not depend on a mains electricity supply. Some of those 1954 recordings were issued on one of the earliest 78rpm records. Since then I had travelled many thousands of miles around Europe and into Asia, mostly by train, in search of the remaining sounds of the steam age. I used more than 400 miles of tape to record those sounds and produced 138 records of various types. A few of those records were never issued and many more have been deleted, but, at the time of writing in 1979, 49 Transacord records remain in the Argo catalogue.

All the earlier recordings were made purely for personal interest and that personal interest remained, even when the issue and sale of records provided an excuse to increase the number and scope of the recordings to an extent undreamed of originally. Certainly it is most satisfying that so many people have enjoyed and still enjoy listening to records of railway sounds. Even if no records had ever been issued, the whole project would have been worthwhile for its own sake, mainly because the recordings made it possible to see so much of the world of railways and involved many vividly memorable experiences for which I shall always be grateful.

# Chapter 7
# The art of railway recording

Since the 1950s, when the first Transacord railway recordings were made on tape and issued on 78rpm discs, both the railways and the equipment used for sound recording have completely changed. The enormous changes on the railways, such as the indecently rapid disappearance of steam locomotives and the destruction of all too many once busy and useful lines, have been of little benefit to railway enthusiasts, or to prospective passengers whose railway or station no longer exists. In contrast, the changes in recording equipment have been wholly beneficial to sound recordists, both amateur and professional, although the ever increasing rate of change sometimes makes it alarmingly difficult to keep up with the latest developments, such as the revolutionary method of digital recording.

Some of the changes which have occurred during the past 25 years are exemplified by the variety of equipment which has been used for making the Transacord railway recordings. Mono recorders were: Excel, made by Excel Sound Services of Bradford, Ferrograph, Vortexion, EMI TR50, and EMI TR51, all of which required an AC mains supply, and EMI L2 and Nagra portable recorders, operating from internal dry batteries. Borrowed Levers Rich mono recorders were also used occasionally. Stereo recorders were: Ferrograph, EMI TR52, EMI TR90, and Revox, all of which required an AC mains supply, and a transportable recorder, custom-built by Stage Sound Ltd, using an EMI tape transport, operated by self contained rechargeable batteries. In recent years I have used exclusively the Nagra IV/S portable recorders, powered by dry batteries.

All the recorders were designed, or modified, to record full track mono or two track stereo at a tape speed of 15ips. Any recorders designed for mains operation had to be supplied from a battery/mains converter, driven by heavy duty lead/acid batteries. The rotary converter, used originally, was superseded by a heavy duty synchronous vibrator unit, specifically designed to drive the 50Hz motors of cine cameras, which operated satisfactorily for some years until it was finally replaced by a transistorised inverter.

I have used a wide variety of microphones, including Western Electric and STC, RCA, Reslo, AKG, Beyer, Electrovoice, and Sennheiser. I have generally preferred dynamic microphones, of various types and characteristics, for railway location recordings, because they are more rugged and less liable to be affected by climatic conditions than the more delicate condenser microphones which, although their frequency response and sensitivity is often superior, have the additional disadvantage of needing an external power supply, except in the case of electret types. Condenser microphones of various types are, however, widely used for film production recording since their superior sensitivity can then be a great advantage.

Now that comparatively simple and inexpensive portable recorders are so widely used, much of the mystique of sound recording has disappeared, just as it vanished from photography, years earlier, when roll film cameras were introduced and photographers ceased hiding under a black cloth. It is no longer necessary for a sound recordist to burden himself with masses of heavy and cumbersome equipment and a move to a new location, which would have occupied endless precious time in earlier years, is now almost as quick and simple for a recordist as it is for a photographer.

Although the equipment has changed greatly the basic principles and technique remain much the same. Recording, like photography, is a combination of art and science; the science can be readily learnt but much of the art is intuitive, not easily taught and best learnt by experiment and experience. Results, of a sort, may quite easily be achieved with a camera or a recorder, but the making of good recordings demands just as much care, attention and imagination as the taking of good photographs.

Anybody who is seriously interested in recording, but lacks

background knowledge, will find it interesting and helpful to read one of the standard works on the subject. One of the best and most comprehensive is *The Manual of Sound Recording,* by John Aldred, published by Fountain Press. The book starts from basic sound and electronic principles and covers every aspect of mono, stereo and multi-track recording, on tape, disc and film; it also includes practical advice on technique, such as the selection and positioning of microphones and descriptions of many types of equipment.

Recording is a more esoteric and indeterminable art than photography; there is equal scope for individualistic approach and no two sound recordists will interpret a subject in exactly the same way. A professional recordist usually sets out to produce a result which is personally pleasing and satisfying, but if that result does not satisfy the customer it will be necessary to make such modifications, however vague, as may be demanded. The scientific element of any method of recording imposes limitations, but the scientific approach should never overrule the artistic, and professional recordists may sometimes consciously ignore some of the rules in an attempt to achieve a certain result. The rules must, however, be learnt before they are broken, since to ignore them without being aware of the possible consequences can easily lead to total disaster.

The best way to learn what can and cannot be done is to experiment, but such opportunities are often denied to professionals since experiments can take time and cost money, expenditure of which customers often begrudge. The amateur has an enormous advantage as having no customer to worry about he can experiment at will until he achieves a personally satisfying result.

Documentary recording on location is inherently more demanding than work in a studio where, within the limitations of a set-up, conditions can be controlled and there is usually an opportunity for rehearsal and even the possibility of a retake if something goes wrong. On location the situation is usually quite different; both the location and the subject may be totally unfamiliar and conditions may be impossible to control, except, to a limited extent, by a reasoned selection of microphone types and positions. Such decisions may have to be made quickly, without benefit of any rehearsal and if the final results are satisfactory it is often more by luck than judgement.

Railway locomotives and trains are by no means easy subjects to record under any circumstances, as anybody who has attempted it will know. The sounds of railway trains have an extremely wide frequency and dynamic range, which can be greater than those of a full symphony orchestra, and it is usually impossible to know quite what to expect from a locomotive. For example a sudden shrill whistle, an unexpected hiss of steam or a startling crescendo of slipping wheels can so easily ruin an otherwise perfect recording, either by overload distortion, or by masking or intermodulating other sounds.

In order to accommodate such a wide range of sound levels it is essential carefully to limit, or boost, the recording level, sometimes to a greater extent than that which may be considered theoretically desirable. Apart from the need to control recording levels it may, less obviously, sometimes be helpful to control the frequency range during recording. For example, the sounds heard on a moving train, or on the footplate of a locomotive, include a considerable amount of extremely low frequencies, the level of which can be usefully reduced by the use of a microphone of limited bass response, or by a bass cut filter, or a combination of both. There is little point in recording a high level of low frequency sounds, since they are unlikely to be effectively reproduced on an average reproducing system, and in any case contribute little to the information and atmosphere conveyed by a recording. The optimum amount of bass cut can ultimately only be determined by experience and it is dangerous to rely on a decision based only on the quality of sound when monitoring on headphones, since they are notoriously unreliable for judging low frequency balance. If in doubt it is safest to cut bass sparingly, since excessive reduction may produce an unpleasantly thin and gutless result and it is easier to cut bass later on than to attempt to restore it.

The cutting of high frequencies during recording is not usually desirable, but may occasionally be helpful in certain extreme cases, such as hissing steam or the squealing of wheels on a curve, where an excess of very high frequencies may restrict the permissible overall recording level to a considerable extent. The judicious use of appropriate filters can also be most helpful in reducing unwanted extraneous background noise, but it is generally better to experiment with various treatments later on than to attempt it when making the original recording.

The choice of recorders suitable for railway location recordings is now extremely wide and the final choice can only be made from personal preference and with consideration for the results required. For anybody intending to start recording with no previous experience it seems unwise to choose anything too complex at first and certainly it is always unwise to rely on the claims of some advertisements which, by using vague references and juggling figures, can imply that an inexpensive domestic recorder is capable of a performance equal to, or better than costly professional equipment. It is primarily essential to choose a recorder capable of producing results which sound satisfyingly good when played back on whatever equipment is to be used for final listening. To judge from the experience of listening to many recordings submitted to record companies it seems obvious that many of them have, previously, only been heard on the recorder on which the recording was made, or on equipment of limited quality. Under such conditions the recording quality may seem acceptable, but when played on equipment of a higher standard all manner of faults become apparent; examples include incorrect azimuth adjustment, uneven tape transit, poor frequency response, overload distortion, hum pick up, motor noise and tape defects. It is a reasonable generalisation that a good recording, made on high quality equipment will sound good when played back on any equipment, but a recording made on inferior equipment, which may sound acceptable when played back over equipment of the same standard, may well sound much less acceptable when played back on higher quality equipment. Therefore, if there is a likelihood that recordings may be listened to on high quality equipment it is worthwhile using a recorder of a reasonably high standard, otherwise the results may seem disappointing.

The main choice of types is between reel to reel and cassette

127

recorders. The performance of modern cassette recorders, especially the best of them, is something which would have been considered quite impossible not so many years ago; since such high quality recordings are now possible on cassette, the small size and weight and consequent portability and convenience may seem to make a cassette recorder the obvious choice for the amateur recordist, but there are some disadvantages. The smaller area of the sound track and the slow speed of recording make a cassette recording more liable to suffer from 'drop outs' due to tape defects or dirt, or to variations in track alignment caused by faulty tape transit. Moreover, cassettes are more liable than tape reels to suffer from mechanical troubles which, like the other faults, always seem to occur at the most vitally inconvenient moments.

Another disadvantage of cassettes is that they are difficult to edit; the slow recording speed makes it hard to locate an accurate cutting point and the small size of the tape makes it difficult to handle. Obviously neither a reel to reel nor cassette tape can be edited if the full width of the tape has been used for recording in both directions, and for that reason and to improve the signal to noise ratio, professional recorders use the full width of the tape for recording in one direction only, whether the recording is mono, two track stereo or multi-track. Editing may, at first thought, seem unimportant, but in fact it is usually most desirable to edit a location recording, otherwise it may soon become boring after the first one or two hearings, especially to anybody other than the recordist. For example, when recording a train starting from a station it is usual to have the recorder on for some time before the train is due to start, in order to ensure that the first whistle and such interesting background sounds as a signal arm changing position are all recorded. However, between such interesting sounds, and in other instances like shunting operations, there may be some unwanted noises, or long silences which, if not removed, will make the recording seem so interminable that the listener will soon be bored and cease to concentrate. Rough editing is, of course, quite possible on cassettes, and cassette recordings can be transferred to $\frac{1}{4}$ inch tape for editing. The larger dimensions of $\frac{1}{4}$ inch tape make it simpler to handle and at higher recording speeds it is easier to locate and mark exact editing points.

Tape editing, quite apart from its most obvious uses, can be a fascinatingly rewarding exercise; the editing of recordings for commercial records and for film sound tracks has become a specialised and somewhat exclusive fine art and it is interesting to discover for yourself just how much can be achieved by practice.

The choice of microphones is now so wide that decisions on which to use can be difficult; the claims of certain advertisements should, like those for recorders, be treated with some caution and, like the selection of headphones or loudspeakers, the final choice will be largely influenced by personal preferences. The first consideration, obviously, is that the microphone must be entirely compatible with the recorder and it is useless to select for example, a low impedance microphone for use with a recorder designed to accept only high impedance microphones. It is not necessary to choose the most sensitive types of microphones for the making of railway recordings; in fact such a choice can at times be quite wrong. An over sensitive microphone may easily be severely overloaded by a close, loud sound which will result in horrible and incurable distortion. A less sensitive and, incidentally, less expensive, microphone used in the same conditions might have been able to cope with the loudest sounds without distortion.

A keen photographer is unlikely to restrict himself to the use of a single type of lens and a recordist would be unwise to rely on only one type of microphone, since each type has characteristic advantages, and the final choice will be dictated by various conditions for each recording. It is often preferable to use omni-directional microphones to give wide coverage of an open location at the lineside, but at a large and busy station it is an advantage to use directional microphones, such as cardioid types, which can usefully reduce the recorded level of unwanted background noise. It must be realised, however, that such microphones are generally less directional to sounds of lower frequencies. When directional microphones are used they must, obviously, be panned to follow a moving object and this cannot always be done easily when working single handed.

The positioning of microphones is of the utmost importance for successful recording, and although useful general guidance is given in text books, there are no absolutely definite rules. A great many factors including the surroundings, the weather conditions, possible sources of unwanted background noise, and the speed at which the train is likely to be travelling, must all be carefully considered, and ultimately a personal decision must be made, based largely on previous experience and modified by the prevailing conditions. If previous experience is lacking a great deal can be gained by experimenting with different types of microphone, used in various positions, in the widest possible variety of locations.

Avoid, if possible, placing microphones too close to the track when recording passing trains; a more distant position will generally give a smoother and more satisfying result, because the recording level will not have to be so sharply reduced to accommodate the sudden peak of sound from the passing train. Another disadvantage of close positioning is that the sounds of the locomotive will probably be completely obscured for some time by the sounds of the rolling stock.

When recording from a train it is usually advantageous to use directional microphones, the optimum position for which is just inside an open window at a point where, according to aerodynamic laws, the air currents are minimal and a microphone can pick up outside sounds without being buffeted by wind. Try to choose a window which is likely to be on the lee side of the train during the journey because, apart from the reduced possibility of wind noise, the sounds of the locomotive are carried by wind to a surprising extent and will be heard best from the lee side of the train. Sometimes it is possible to achieve good results from microphones placed right outside the train, but even with the most efficient wind shields, which are obviously necessary, there is a risk that the microphone diaphragm may be at least partially paralysed by wind in extreme conditions. A further disadvantage of completely exterior positioning is that the results may be somewhat unrealistic from the point of view of a passenger who might expect to hear a more familiar balance of sounds. All too often, though, there is a lot of unwanted background noise on a train and if it is impossible to find a suitable and uncrowded window, there may be no alternative to using an exterior microphone position. It will certainly be better than nothing and for some parts of the journey at least, the results may well be perfectly satisfying.

Weather conditions are of enormous importance in exterior locations; wind strength and direction are totally unpredictable problems and it is always essential to be prepared for the worst. It is foolhardy to attempt any exterior recording, even on the calmest day, without the insurance of at least a light windshield on the microphone. A light breeze, blowing up unexpectedly at a vital moment, or the turbulence set up by a passing train, may ruin an otherwise perfect recording if the microphone is unprotected. Windshields of varying design and efficiency are supplied by most microphone manufacturers. The fabric covered types are generally the most efficient, but are usually large, can be costly and are not available for all types and makes of microphone; the cheaper windshields, which are moulded from a special plastic foam of known acoustic properties, are widely available, easily fitted and give adequate protection in average situations. The indiscriminate swathing of microphones in layers of ordinary foam of unknown acoustic properties is certainly not recommended, but an effective windshield can be quite easily made at little cost. The essential principle is a cage which must completely surround the microphone and be separated from it; the whole cage is then covered in a fine meshed, silky material, such as ladies' tights. Ideally two separated layers of material should be used and to a certain extent the efficiency is increased by enlarging the size of the cage, within practical limits. Windshields constructed from various sizes of soup strainers, covered with separated layers of nylon stocking material, were used with various types of microphones for many years, both for film location and railway recordings and invariably proved effective in some of the most adverse conditions in exposed locations.

If a windshield is not giving adequate protection in exceptionally windy conditions it may be helpful to change to a different type of microphone; for instance, sensitive condenser microphones are notoriously affected by wind noise to a far greater extent than dynamic types. The shape and size of a microphone can also be a significant factor; a smaller microphone will usually be less physically affected by wind and it may also be inherently less susceptible to wind noise because some small microphones have a poor bass response. In extreme conditions the only solution may be to use such a microphone and although the quality of the resulting recording may be somewhat thin, it will be preferable to a fuller quality recording overlaid by heavy bouts of wind noise and certainly much better than no recording at all. Buildings, walls and even hedges may provide useful shelter for microphones, but such objects also set up echoes which may be troublesome or helpful and must always be considered. An obvious disadvantage of sheltering microphones in such a way is that they may also be screened from wanted wind borne sounds and consequently a recording made in such circumstances can be all too brief, though better than nothing. It is quite useless sheltering microphones near trees because the noise of the wind in the trees, which is always more apparent to any microphone than to the optimistically selective human ear, will probably ruin the recording anyway. In extreme conditions it can be worth experimenting with microphones in a low position, a few inches from the ground, but remember that wind blowing through heather, shrubs, or long grass can produce an astonishing amount of hiss, which will be unfailingly recorded at an irritatingly high level if the microphone is closely surrounded by such herbage. It is also possible that some strange and unpredictable changes in sound quality may occur when microphones are used in unconventionally low positions. It is always worth experimenting while waiting for conditions to improve, for some surprisingly interesting results can be achieved in seemingly impossible conditions.

Rain is one of the worst problems, quite apart from the discomfort which it causes and the well known incompatibility of electronic equipment and damp. A steady drizzle or light rain is merely uncomfortable, so long as the equipment can be kept dry and provided that the microphone windshield does not become saturated. Heavy rain will cause excessively loud plops and thuds if it falls on a windshield of any type and in such conditions the microphone must be protected by a rain shield, made from some heavy material such as felt or thick foam and secured as far as possible above the microphone, consistent with protection. Ordinary umbrellas are worse than useless as microphone rain shields because the patter of rain falling on the taut surface will be clearly heard.

For stereophonic recordings there are a number of different conventions concerning the relationship between the microphones, and a decision on which to adopt must be a matter of personal choice, based on experience and on the prevailing conditions. Provided that the important principles of stereo recording are always considered there is no need to stick to rigid rules. The placing of the microphones for the stereo recording of *The Triumph of an A4 Pacific* was highly unconventional, especially at the time, but, nevertheless, produced results which critics and others considered realistic.

The correct positioning of microphones for stereo recordings on exterior locations is not a simple matter, particularly where trains moving over a wide stretch of varying surroundings are concerned. In such circumstances it is almost inevitable that, no matter where or how the microphones are placed, some phase differences will occur at one or more points during the recording, because as the train moves across the landscape its sounds will be variously reflected from the surroundings. The major fault of a 'hole in the middle' effect as the train goes past at the nearest point can, however, be avoided by choice of suitable microphones and by carefully positioning them with regard to nearby objects, such as buildings or woods, which may throw back echoes that can cause complete or partial cancellation of sounds at various frequencies, leading to some very strange results.

Stereo recordings are invariably best made with the microphones on a stand or a boom arm in a fixed position; some extraordinary and unwelcome results can occur if stereo microphones are moved during a recording and it is more satisfactory to let the subject do the moving than to pan the microphones.

When recording for film production there is a constant problem of compromise between placing microphones in an optimum position for recording, and concealing them from the camera, so a number of microphones are set up in various positions and used through a mixer, individually or in combinations of two or more, as appropriate. A similar technique has been used for railway recordings from time to time, particularly when equipment used to be so cumbersome that it could not easily or quickly be moved, but the multi-microphone method is inherently cumbersome and the possibility of technical problems obviously increases if additional equipment is used. It is always an anxious moment when a remote microphone is faded in and this anxiety is considerably increased when working on film productions, for which it is now common practice to use a number of radio microphones which are notoriously prone to develop sudden strange faults. If a suitably static set-up can be arranged for railway recordings it is sometimes possible to achieve most interesting results by using a number of microphones with a mixer, always provided that the result can be monitored on headphones, but if such monitoring facilities are not available it is obviously pointless to attempt to use a mixer. Generally it is preferable to take advantage of the mobility of modern equipment and to change positions whenever it may seem necessary, rather than be burdened with a mixer and numerous microphones with cables, so inconveniently liable to tangle, running in all directions.

The choice of lineside locations, so obviously important, is often far from easy. Maps, such as the Ordnance Survey, are most helpful, but they cannot give all the essential information, and, before making an important 'one chance only' recording, a location reconnaissance is well worthwhile, if at all possible, to select in advance the positions most likely to be the most satisfactory for various conditions of weather and wind direction. Careful and intelligent choice of locations greatly increase the chances of success, but all too often there are last minute problems with noise from such unpredictable sources as aircraft, road traffic, not heard until the wind changes direction, or a tractor, which appears over a hill and starts working ever closer backwards and forwards across an enormous field; perhaps most inappropriate of all are noisy spectators and transistor radios. Sometimes such things as bridges, walls, cutting sides and embankments can be surprisingly effective as baffles between the microphone and unwanted noises; it may be helpful to use directional microphones, but the intrusive sound is often reflected from an object in front of the microphone, partly nullifying its directional advantages. Although highly directional microphones can reduce background noise, they may also produce an exceptionally dead and clinically unrealistic recording which is uninspiring and possibly boring to hear more than once.

Lineside telegraph wires are often troublesome for they may be completely silent for hours, then suddenly start humming at a most inopportune moment. If the microphone is anywhere near the wires it will unfailingly pick up any humming which, although probably unnoticed while a train goes past, can sound unpleasantly like a serious equipment fault when the sounds of the train diminish as it goes away into the distance. High voltage overhead power lines must always be treated with suspicion and given a reasonably wide berth, because they are usually surrounded by a strong electrical field which, by induction in microphones, cables or the recorder, can create a most unpleasant hum, loud enough to ruin any recording.

Many background sounds will contribute to the atmosphere and reality of railway recordings. The inclusion of such sounds as signal arms, points, whistles and station announcements will, if properly balanced in relation to the sounds of locomotives and trains, greatly increase the interest of a recording. In the country the sounds of animals and birds provide a perfect natural setting for passing trains and are often sufficiently and strongly individualistic to identify a setting in broad terms; for instance on the Settle & Carlisle line, the background sounds in summer or winter, will be quite different from those likely to be heard beside a line in Southern England. Natural sounds are, however, not always helpful; it was, for example, never possible for me to find entirely suitable recording positions anywhere beside the Brecon & Merthyr line on the famous seven mile, 925ft climb between Talybont on Usk and Torpantau. To judge from maps it appeared to be a superbly suitable, remote location, but in fact was plagued by aircraft, swooping up and down the valley which was filled with rushing streams and waterfalls. They could be heard for considerable distances and created a continuous background noise, normally pleasant, but in these circumstances most unwelcome, because the sounds of the trains themselves were masked, or interfered with, to such an extent that the majority of recordings made in the area had to be rejected. When judging the amount and type of background noise which may be acceptable in a recording, it must always be remembered that ears are selective but microphones are not. A background of noise which may seem acceptable to the ear will consequently often turn out to be totally unacceptable in a recording, particularly if it is listened to some time later, without the support of a visual image.

Sound recording as a profession has much to commend it; each new problem keeps interest alive in a search for a solution and there is, even now, a certain mystery attached to the making of recordings. It still tends to be a somewhat secretive process, perhaps because a recordist spends so much time wearing headphones which isolate him from the outside world and by so doing may, all too easily, induce a possibly dangerously introspective outlook. Sound recording as a pastime can be immensely rewarding and can even be a therapeutic antidote to various stresses in much the same way as can fishing, other than match angling. Location recording has some similarities to fishing, with long periods of preparation and waiting, during which there is ample opportunity to observe and enjoy the surroundings, followed by the possible disappointment of a missed opportunity or the excitement of the catch of a successful and satisfying recording.

There are still plenty of opportunities for interesting recordings of railway sounds, particularly in Britain with so many preserved lines and steam-hauled special trains. Other countries too have preserved lines and run steam-hauled specials

136

while, further afield, it is possible to find steam locomotives still in commercial service. Even diesel locomotives are not without interest, now that so many individual types are disappearing much sooner than had been expected. It is doubtful whether any diesel locomotive can ever have the same individuality and personality as a steam locomotive and they most certainly cannot produce anything like the same variety of fascinating sounds. Nevertheless many of the withdrawn or threatened diesel locomotive classes do already have strong supporters' clubs.

Changes on the railways and elsewhere take place at a seemingly ever increasing rate and if there are any sounds now which interest or inspire you it is surely worthwhile recording them before they disappear. It is a thoroughly unpleasant thought but, considering the nature and rate of recent changes, it is by no means impossible that even some of those railways which are still with us now could, all too easily and all too soon, become nothing more than a memory.

# Discography

Serial numbers were allocated to several records which, for various reasons, were either not completed or were never issued, therefore there are some breaks in the sequence of the 10 inch Transacord records.

The Argo Transacord record catalogue numbers are shared with other Argo records and consequently catalogue numbers of records produced by Transacord for Argo do not necessarily follow in sequence.

**Records issued independently by Transacord Limited, between November 1955 and November 1961 and sold only by direct mail order.** *All deleted by December 1961.*

**10 inch 78rpm records**

| | |
|---|---|
| E/426–7 | FREIGHT TRAINS |
| E/428–9 | BIRMINGHAM–LEAMINGTON |
| E/440–1 | THE CLASS A3 PACIFIC LOCOMOTIVE |
| E/442–3 | FROM LONDON (EUSTON) |
| E/444–5 | VENICE–MESTRE |
| E/451–2 | THE LICKEY INCLINE–FREIGHT TRAINS |
| E/453–4 | THE LICKEY INCLINE–PASSENGER TRAINS |
| E/455–6 | THE KING CLASS LOCOMOTIVE |

**10 inch 33⅓rpm LP records**

| | |
|---|---|
| 5021–2 | THE BULLEID PACIFIC LOCOMOTIVE |
| 5023–4 | THE CLASS A4 PACIFIC LOCOMOTIVE |
| 5025–6 | THE DUKEDOGS |
| 5030–1 | VICTORIA–CHATHAM |
| 5032–3 | THE LICKEY INCLINE |
| 5034–5 | THE WATLINGTON BRANCH |
| 5036–7 | THE LNW 0–8–0 |
| 5038–9 | SOUNDS OF SHUNTING |
| 5040–1 | GREAT CENTRAL |
| 5042–3 | CASTLES |
| 5044–5 | KINGS |
| 5046–7 | A3 PACIFICS |
| 5048–9 | ON THE FOOTPLATE |
| 5050–1 | THE MIDLAND COMPOUND |
| 5052–3 | TRAMWAY SOUNDS |

**7 inch 33⅓rpm records**

c/1000–1    EDWARD'S DAY OUT and EDWARD AND GORDON. Railway stories, narrated by the author, the Reverend Awdry, with sound effects. Produced for and issued by Chiltern Records Ltd.

1002–3    LICKEY 1955

1004–5    BULLEID PACIFICS

**12 inch 33⅓rpm LP records. Originally issued independently by Transacord; re-cut, re-pressed and re-issued by Argo, with new and improved sleeves, in November 1961.**

6000–1    THE WEST HIGHLAND LINE

6002–3    SHAP

6004–5    SOMERSET AND DORSET

**Transacord 7 inch extended play 45rpm records issued by Argo but now deleted and no longer available. Argo catalogue numbers and titles.**

*(Some of these recordings have been, or will be, electronically re-processed and re-issued on LP records in the Argo SPA 'World of Railways' series.)*

EAF 33    GRESLEY PACIFICS

EAF 34    N7 ON THE JAZZ

EAF 35    SOUTH EASTERN STEAM

EAF 36    NARROW GAUGE ON THE COSTA BRAVA

EAF 37    DUKEDOGS AND THE CITY

EAF 38    STEAM TRACTION ENGINES

EAF 39    JEANIE DEANS AND OXFORD (Clyde and Thames Steamers)

EAF 43    SOUTH WESTERN STEAM

EAF 59    ON THE ABERDEEN FLYER

EAF 70    HUNTS, SHIRES AND SANDRINGHAMS

EAF 71    G5s ON THE PUSH AND PULL

EAF 72    THE 11.15 FOR TORPANTAU

EAF 73    WITH 'THE MAIL' TO AVIEMORE

EAF 74    CALEDONIAN ENGINES

EAF 75    ON THE FOOTPLATE OF A KING

EAF 76    THE SOUTHERN SCHOOLS

EAF 77    PACIFIC POWER

EAF 78    THE GLENFIELD GOODS

EAF 79    THE SNOWDON MOUNTAIN RAILWAY

EAF 80    GREAT NORTHERN ENGINES

EAF 81    GRANGES AND MANORS

EAF 82    THE ATLANTICS AND THE TERRIER

EAF 83    NORTH EASTERN ENGINES

EAF 84    CASTLES IN THE CHILTERNS

EAF 86    GRANTHAM, 1957

EAF 88    STANIER PACIFICS

EAF 87    BULLEID PACIFICS

| | |
|---|---|
| EAF 97 | TRAINS ON THE NARROW GAUGE |
| EAF 98 | D FOR DIESELS |
| EAF 99 | LNW ENGINES |
| EAF 116 | GREAT CENTRAL ENGINES |
| EAF 100 | TWO CASTLES FROM PLYMOUTH |
| EAF 117 | TRAINS IN TROUBLE |
| EAF 118 | ENGINES ON THE CONTINENT |
| EAF 119 | THE SOUNDS OF SHUNTING |
| EAF 121 | TRAMWAY SOUNDS |
| EAF 127 | MIDLAND ENGINES |
| EAF 124 | THE O2 TANKS |
| EAF 125 | CHANGE AT TEMPLECOMBE |
| EAF 126 | THE HIGHLANDERS |
| EAF 128 | PANNIERS AND PRAIRIES |
| EAF 129 | ROYAL SCOTS AND JUBILEES |
| EAF 130 | THIS IS YORK |
| EAF 131 | TRAINS FROM TYNE DOCK |
| EAF 132 | THE BRITANNIAS AND THE CLANS |
| EAF 135 | SOUTHERN ENGINES |
| EAF 136 | DOUBLE HEADED |
| EAF 137 | KINGS IN THE CHILTERNS |
| EAF 138 | ON A BANKER FROM BEATTOCK |
| EAF 139 | MIXED TRAIN TO ROSPORDEN |
| EAF 140 | INDUSTRIAL ENGINES |
| EAF 141 | THE WDs |
| EAF 144 | EXHIBITIONIST ENGINES |
| EAF 145 | LNER PACIFICS |
| EAF 146 | THE SOUNDS OF BRESSINGHAM |
| EAF 148 | NORTH BRITISH ENGINES |
| EAF 149 | STEAM IN THE WORTH VALLEY |
| EAF 150 | THE HALLS |
| EAF 151 | WORTH VALLEY ENGINES |
| EAF 152 | CLUN CASTLE AND KOLHAPUR |

**Argo Transacord recordings**
**Sounds of the Steam Age**
*(For details of record sizes and speeds etc see code at end).*

TR 101   THE WEST HIGHLAND LINE
Steam locomotives of the former NBR, LNER and LMS, at work at various
locations on the West Highland line, during winter and spring, in the
1950s.

TR 102   SHAP
Ex LMS and other steam locomotives, heard from the lineside, at various
locations between Tebay and Shap Summit, between 1958 and 1960.

TR 103   THE SOMERSET AND DORSET
Steam locomotives of various types, at work on the S&D line, at different
locations between Evercreech Junction and Masbury in 1956 and a

journey on the double headed Pines Express, between Bath and Evercreech Junction.

## TR 104   WEST OF EXETER
Ex GWR steam locomotives, of various classes, heard from the lineside at Dainton and Exeter and from inside the signal boxes at Tigley and Exeter, in 1957 and 1958.

## ZTR 105   TRAINS IN THE NIGHT
Steam hauled trains in the night, in winter and summer, in 1959, 1961 and 1962, at Bromsgrove, on the GW&GC line, on the Central Wales line and on the Carlisle–Edinburgh line.

## ZTR 106   NEWFOUNDLAND HEADS THE WAVERLEY
A journey on the Waverley Express, hauled by Jubilee 4-6-0 *Newfoundland*, between Hellifield and Blea Moor and lineside recordings at Dent and Ribblehead, in 1960.

## TR 107   THE GREAT EASTERN
Steam locomotives of various ex Great Eastern classes, at work on Great Eastern lines in the 1950s.

## ZTR 108   THE TRIUMPH OF AN A4 PACIFIC
A journey on the SLS special train, headed by *Sir Nigel Gresley* driven by Bill Hoole, on the record breaking run between Kings Cross and Doncaster and Kings Cross, in May 1959.

## ZTR 109   TRAINS IN THE HILLS
Steam locomotives of the London Midland and Western regions, heard from the lineside at Shap, Blea Moor, Abergavenny and on the Lickey Incline.

## ZTR 113   RHYTHMS OF STEAM
Steam locomotives, of various types, heard from the lineside, at Tyndrum, Tyne Dock, Hitchin, Templecombe, Montrose, and Barkston Junction. A journey on a special train, hauled by the Midland Compound 4-4-0, No 1000.

## TR 114   WORKING ON THE FOOTPLATE
Journeys on the footplate of four steam locomotives. An A4 Pacific with Aberdeen–Glasgow express, a V2 2-6-2 with an Edinburgh–Dundee freight train, a Class 5 4-6-0 with a Swansea–Shrewsbury passenger train and an 8F 2-8-0 with a Shrewsbury–Swansea freight train.

## ZTR 115   THE POWER OF STEAM
Steam locomotives of various types, heard from the lineside at Ardlui, Scout Green, Basingstoke, Minnavey Colliery, Bargany, on the Lickey Incline and on the Carlisle–Edinburgh line.

### TR 117　THE GREAT WESTERN
Various classes of ex Great Western steam locomotives, heard from the lineside at Hatton, Abergavenny, Chalford, Princes Risborough and Evershot.

### ZTR 118　TRAINS TO REMEMBER ●KZTC 118
Steam hauled trains remembered. During a night at Grantham Station, on the Scarborough–Whitby–Pickering line, on the Central Wales line, on the Lickey Incline, on the Stranraer–Ayr line and at Talerddig Station.

### ZTR 121　ECHOES OF ENGINES ●KZTC 121
Steam locomotives at work during an evening, night and morning at Gresford. At Montrose, Okehampton and on the Carlisle–Edinburgh line. Inside the signal box at Meldon Junction.

### ZTR 123　COPPER CAPPED ENGINES
Various ex GWR steam locomotives at work at Talerddig, Basingstoke, Llanvihangel, Princes Risborough, Gresford and Evershot Tunnel.

### TR 124　VIVE LA VAPEUR
SNCF steam locomotives of various types at Breaute, Beuzeville, Argentan, St Germain des Fosses and Eygurande. A steam hauled journey on a steeply graded line in Auvergne.

### ZTR 125　THE KNOTTY
A musical documentary which, in words, songs and sounds, tells the story of early railway days, from the stage coach to the amalgamation. Adapted from Peter Cheeseman's production at the Victoria Theatre, Stoke on Trent.

### ZTR 126　THE RAILWAY TO RICCARTON
Steam locomotives of various ex LNER types, at work on the steeply graded Carlisle–Edinburgh line, the Waverley route, between Newcastleton and Hawick, in the spring of 1961.

### ZTR 128　STEAM ON THE LICKEY INCLINE
Steam locomotives of various types, working goods and passenger trains on the Lickey Incline, between Bromsgrove and Blackwell, in 1959.

### ZTR 129　ENGINES ON THE BUNDESBAHN
Steam locomotives of various types, working goods and passenger trains at many different locations on the DB, in West Germany in 1970.

### TR 130　ORIENT EXPRESS
A steam hauled journey on the Orient Express through the Balkans to Istanbul. Steam locomotives of Yugoslavia, Bulgaria, Greece and Turkey heard from the train and from the lineside, en route.

# DISCOGRAPHY

**ZTR 131   TRAINS IN THE FIFTIES**
Steam locomotives at work on BR, in the closing years of the 1950s. At Hitchin, Durham, Abergavenny, Beattock, Basingstoke and Llangunllo.

**TR 134   NORTH OF KINGS CROSS**
A variety of ex LNER steam locomotives, at work in the 1950s and in 1961. At Kings Cross, Hitchin, Peterborough, Stoke Tunnel, Retford, Edinburgh and Whitrope.

**ZTR 138   ENGINES IN GERMANY**
East German and West German Pacific locomotives and various other steam locomotive types, at work on the DB in West Germany. A companion record to ZTR 129 *Engines on the Bundesbahn.*

**TR 140   ENGINES FROM DERBY AND CREWE**
Steam locomotives of a variety of ex LMS types, at work at many different locations on British Railways, during the years between 1955 and 1965.

**ZTR 143   RAILWAYS ROUND THE CLOCK**
Steam locomotives at work on British Railways, by day and night, at Gresford, Templecombe, Ribblehead, Barkston Junction and Scout Green. A footplate journey, on a Britannia Pacific, on the Ayr–Stranraer line.

**ZTR 148   STEAM IN ALL DIRECTIONS ●KZTC 148**
Steam locomotives of many different types, at work on railways in England, Scotland, Wales, Germany, Italy, Romania and Yugoslavia.

**ZTR 149   STEAM THROUGH ALL SEASONS**
Steam locomotives at work in the spring, summer, autumn and winter. On British Railways at Barkston Junction, Llanvihangel, Princes Risborough, Bromsgrove, Knucklas and on the climb to Whitrope Summit. One of the famous Maffei Pacifics in Romania, a 2-8-0 in the Dolomites and a 2-10-0 in Germany.

**ZFA 77   PACIFIC POWER**
LNER, LMS, SR and BR Pacifics at work on British Railways.

**ZFA 153   TALYLLYN TRAINS**
Five steam locomotives at work on the narrow gauge Talyllyn Railway in Wales.

**ZFA 154   SOUNDS OF THE FESTINIOG**
Four of the FR steam locomotives at work on the narrow gauge Festiniog Railway, in Wales, with passenger and goods trains.

**The 'World of Railways' records**
SPA 103   THE WORLD OF STEAM ●KCSP 103
Steam locomotives at work on railways in Britain, at Templecombe, on the Paddington–Birmingham line, at Bromsgrove, on the Waverley route and at Shap Summit. On railways abroad, in Spain, Germany and Turkey.

143

# DISCOGRAPHY

**SPA 211    THE WORLD OF STEAM VOL 2**
Steam locomotives at work on railways in Britain, at Basingstoke, near Montrose and at Blea Moor. On railways abroad, in Romania, Yugoslavia, France and Germany.

**SPA 337    THE WORLD OF STEAM VOL 3**
Steam Traction Engines and a Fairground Roundabout Organ, of the Victorian era. On board a Paddle Steamer in Switzerland. Steam locomotives on railways in Italy, Germany and England.

**SPA 438    CHANGING TRAINS ●KCSP 438**
Steam and Diesel locomotives, of various types, at work at different locations on BR between 1957 and 1966. A journey in the cab of the High Speed Train, during a 125mph test run, in February 1975.

**SPA 439    STEAM LOCOMOTION – Rail 150 ●KCSP 439**
The *Locomotion* replica and a variety of other steam locomotives, the majority of which either took part in the Rail 150 Anniversary Cavalcade, or are representative of types exhibited at Shildon, during the 150th Anniversary celebrations.

**SPA 440    GWR ●KCSP 440**
Steam locomotives of various ex GWR classes, at work on BR between 1955 and 1963 at Abergavenny, Dainton, Tigley, Ruabon, Saunderton, Crumlin, Aberystwyth, Talerddig, Princes Risborough and Hatton and on a journey between Totnes and Plymouth.

**SPA 461    GREAT CENTRAL ●KCSP 461**
Steam locomotives of the former GCR and LNER lines at work on former Great Central and other lines on British Railways, during the 1950s.

**SPA 462    SOUTHERN STEAM ●KCSP 462**
Steam locomotives of many ex Southern Railway classes at work at various locations on BR with goods and passenger trains, in the 1950s.

**SPA 463 LMS ●KCSP 463**
Steam locomotives of the former LMS at work on BR at Euston Station in 1955. At Blea Moor, Ribblehead, Marsden and Bromsgrove. On the climb to Shap Summit. On the Abergavenny–Merthyr line and between Perth and Gleneagles.

**SPA 499    VAPEUR EN FRANCE ●KCSP 499**
Steam locomotives of various classes, at work on the SNCF and other lines, in Northern, Central and Southern France, between 1959 and 1975.

**SPA 506    LNER ●KCSP 506**
Steam locomotives of the London & North Eastern Railway, at work on British Railways between 1956 and 1961 at Grantham, Peterborough, Whitrope Summit and Hitchin.

**SPA 529    THIS IS YORK ●KCSP 529**
The sounds of a great station: York during the steam age, in 1957 and with diesel traction, including Inter City 125 in 1977, the centenary year of the present station.

**SPA 530    A DOUBLE HEAD OF STEAM ●KCSP 530**
Steam locomotives, with passenger and goods trains, mostly double headed, at many different locations on British Railways, between 1956 and 1966. The GNR Atlantic *Henry Oakley* with double headed trains on the KWVR in 1977.

**SPA 557    CASTLES AND KINGS ●KCSP 557**
GWR Castle class and King class 4-6-0 locomotives at work on British Railways between 1956 and 1967 at Hatton, Bristol Temple Meads, Dainton Tunnel, Coton Hill, Sapperton, in the Chiltern Hills, at Exeter St Davids, and on the footplate of *King Edward VIII*.

**SPA 563    PACIFIC POWER ●KCSP 563**
LNER, LMS, SR and BR Pacifics at work on BR between 1956 and 1976; including most of the recordings previously issued on the EP ZFA 77, with other recordings not previously issued. SNCF, DB, and DR Pacifics at work in France and in Germany.

**SPA 564    TRAINS IN TROUBLE ●KCSP 564**
Steam locomotives in various kinds of difficulties, with passenger and goods trains, on British Railways and in Austria and Yugoslavia.

**SPA 572    MIDLAND AND NORTH WESTERN ●KCSP 572**
Steam locomotives of the Midland, London & North Western and LMS railways at work at various locations on BR between 1955 and 1975.

TR = 12 inch LP Mono recording
ZTR = 12 inch LP Stereo recording
ZFA = 7 inch EP Stereo recording
SPA = 12 inch LP Stereo or electronically re-processed stereo recordings
●KZTC and KCSP = stereo cassettes, these are available for all records indicated by the addition of ●cassette numbers.

# Index

DB and DR, *see* Germany
DBS, *see* Denmark
D Day, 23, 24
Decca Record Company, 44, 62,
    89-91, 95, 96
demobilisation, from army, 31
Denham, 20, 33
Denmark, 31
diesel motive power, 15, 34, 48,
    91, 92, 98, 99
'Director' 4-4-0 locomotive, 64,
    78
disc recording equipment, 25,
    43-5, 56
'Dukedog' 4-4-0 locomotive, 79
Dutch 0-6-0T locomotive, 26

'E1' 4-4-0 locomotive, 71
Eastern Region BR, *see* LNER
Edinburgh-Carlisle line, *see*
    Waverley route
editing of recordings, 128, 129
'8F' 2-8-0 locomotive, 17, 33, 78,
    79, 84, 111
Eisenhower, General Eisenhower's
    special train, 24
Elstree, 33, 34
end of steam on BR, 48, 59, 99
Euston Stn, 55
Evercreech Junc, 67

films and railways, 7, 16, 37-42,
    47
film sound tracks, 7, 16, 19, 22,
    25-7, 35, 37-43, 46, 53, 54,
    76, 77, 81, 88, 96, 97, 134
'5MT' 4-6-0 locomotive, 24, 33,
    97
Folkestone, 69, 70
footplate journeys, 23, 24, 79, 80,
    92, 97, 104
Forth Bridge, 97
'4300' class 2-6-0 locomotive, 74
Fowler 2-6-4T locomotive, 32
France, 14, 22, 24, 25, 37, 38, 40,
    74, 100-4
French locomotives, 14, 40,
    101-4, 110

frequency response, 126, 127
FS, *see* Italy

'G5' 0-4-4T locomotive, 71
Gale, John, 87, 92
Garratt locomotive, 51, 72, 107,
    108
*Gazelle* S & MR locomotive, 24
GCR 2-8-0 locomotive, 65, 66
Germany, 27-31, 77, 120, 121
Giesl-Gieslingen, Doctor A., 116
Gingell, Sam (driver), 14, 71, 75
'Glen' 4-4-0 locomotive, 81, 82
Glenfield, 97
*Gordon Highlander* 4-4-0
    locomotive, 98
*Gramophone, The,* 83, 87, 91
Grantham, 18, 64, 79, 83
Greece, 109, 110
Greenfield, Edward, 91
Gresford, 97
*Gresley Pacifics,* EP record, 91
GW & GC (Great Western & Great
    Central joint line), 20, 21, 34-6,
    43, 48, 56, 64, 91, 92, 98, 99
GWR and BR Western Region, 13,
    21, 32, 36, 42, 43, 48, 74, 75,
    79, 80, 83, 91, 92, 96-9, 136
GWR 2-8-0 locomotive, 21

Hardy, Richard, 71, 100, 101
Hatton, 92
Hitchin, 18, 64, 83, 101
Holland, 26, 27, 29
Hoole, Bill (driver), 14, 82, 83, 96
HR 4-6-0 locomotive No 103, 98

Isle of Wight, 97
Italy, 35, 47, 121, 122

'J15' 0-6-0 locomotive, 20, 71
'J36' 0-6-0 locomotive, 93, 94
Johnson 0-4-4T locomotive, 67
Jones Goods 4-6-0 locomotive, 98
'Jubilee' 4-6-0 locomotive, 34, 84
JZ, *see* Yugoslavia

'K3' 2-6-0 locomotive, 93

North Staffordshire Railway, 62
North Yorkshire Moors Railway,
98
NS, *see* Holland
'N7' 0-6-2T locomotive, 80

OBB, *see* Austria
*Observer,* 87
optical sound recording system,
20, 26, 34, 35, 44
'Orient Express', 39, 40, 47,
109-11, 116
*Orient Express* LP record, 142

'Pacific' locomotives: 'A1', 93;
'A3', 15, 38, 63, 65, 79, 93;
'A4', 16, 38, 63, 72, 79, 82,
83, 93-7; Bulleid, 63, 66;
'Britannia', 79; DB and DR
(German), 121; LMS, 72, 95,
96; Maffei (CFR), 117; SNCF
(France), 101, 102
pannier tank locomotive, 70, 75,
83
*Paris Express* LP record, 107
Paris, liberation of, 25
Peterborough, 65, 101
photography, 12, 16, 23-5, 28-31,
34, 36, 52, 124, 125, 129, *see
also* AFPU
Pinewood Studios, 22
prairie tank locomotive, 96
preserved railways, 41, 98, 99,
136
Preston, 70
Princes Risborough, 34-6, 48, 91,
92, 98, 99

'Q7' 0-8-0 locomotive, 72

*Railway Children, The,* (film), 41
*Railway Magazine,* 57
Rattery and Dainton, 74
RCTS (Railway Correspondence
& Travel Society), 83, 95, 96
recording equipment, *see* disc,
optical, tape, microphones,
mixer

recording equipment, choice of,
127, 128
recording for films, *see* film sound
tracks, films and railways
records, early 78 rpm and LP
issues, 56, 60, 61
records, American railway records,
55, 56, 76
record reviews, *see The
Gramophone*
RENFE, *see* Spain
Renoir, Jean, 38
Reseau Breton, 104
Retford, 65, 66
Rhine, crossing of the, 28
Ribblehead, 16, 83, 84, 94, 95
Romania, 116-20
'Royal Scot' 4-6-0 locomotive, 98

'Schools' 4-4-0 locomotive, 73
Scotland, 75, 76, 81, 82, 92-8
Scottish Region BR, *see* LMS and
LNER
S & DJR 2-8-0 locomotive, 66, 67
S & DJR, Somerset & Dorset line,
66, 67, 83
Settle & Carlisle line, 16, 83, 84,
94, 95, 99, 135
Shap, 10, 16, 74, 77, 83, 92
*Shap* LP record, 87, 91
signal box and signal, sounds of,
13, 15, 128
SLS (Stephenson Locomotive
Society), 76, 82, 95, 96, 98
S & MR (Shropshire &
Montgomeryshire Railway), 24
SNCF, *see* France
*Somerset and Dorset,* LP record,
87, 91
Southern Region BR, *see* SR
Spain, 48, 51, 107, 108
SR and BR Southern Region, 19,
42, 48, 63, 66, 69-71, 73, 75,
83
steam, end of on BR, *see* end of
steam
Steele Road, 92-4
Stephens, Colonel, 24

Stephenson, Brian, 94, 120, 121
stereo, early recordings, 80-3, 91
stereo recording technique, 133

Talerddig, 97
tape-recording equipment, 43-8,
  51, 53, 55, 65, 66, 73, 74,
  79-82, 100, 122, 123
Tay Bridge, 97
TCDD, see Turkey
Templecombe, 18, 66, 67, 83
*This is York* 'World of Railways'
  LP record, 15
'3F' 0-6-0 locomotive, 67
'T9' 4-4-0 locomotive, 72
*Trains Illustrated*, 57
*Trains in the Night* LP record, 91
*Trains to Remember* LP record,
  98
trams, 25, 44
*Triumph of an A4 Pacific*, LP
  record, 82, 133
Turkey, 39, 40, 109-13
'2F' 0-6-0 locomotive, 97
'2P' 4-4-0 locomotive, 67, 74

UNRRA locomotives, 35
Usill, Harley, 89, 90, 96

'V2' 2-6-2 locomotive, 38, 65, 72,
  73, 92, 93, 97
*Vapeur en France* 'World of
  Railways' LP record, 107
*Vive la Vapeur* LP record, 107

Wainwright 'D' 4-4-0 locomotive,
  71
Wales, 17, 18, 32, 33, 74, 76, 79,
  95, 97, 136
Walker, Colin, 75, 96
Watlington branch line, 36, 74
Waverley route, 16, 92-4
'WD' 2-8-0 locomotive, 26
Western Region BR, see GWR
West Highland line, 76, 81, 82
*West Highland Line*, LP record,
  87, 91
*West of Exeter*, LP record, 91
Wilcox, Herbert, 37
Wilmot, Chester, 27
Wimbush, Roger, 61, 83
*Wind in the Willows, The*, LP
  record, 89
*Working on the Footplate*, LP
  record, 97

York Station, 15, 16
Yugoslavia, 40, 109, 110, 114,
  115